1984

Scene Painting

Scene Painting
Tools and Techniques

Daniel Veaner

A SPECTRUM BOOK

Prentice-Hall, Inc., Englewood Cliffs, New Jersey 07632

Library of Congress Cataloging in Publication Data

Veaner, Daniel.
 Scene painting.

 "A Spectrum Book."
 Includes index.
 1. Scene painting — Technique. 2. Artists' tools.
I. Title.
ND2885. V4 1984 750'.28 83-27028
ISBN 0-13-791658-2
ISBN 0-13-791641-8 (pbk.)

10 9 8 7 6 5 4 3 2 1

ISBN 0-13-791658-2

ISBN 0-13-791641-8 {PBK.}

Editorial/production supervision by Norma G. Ledbetter
Color insert design by Susan Maksuta
Page layout by Maria Carella
Cover design by Hal Siegel
Manufacturing buyer: Edward J. Ellis

This book is available at a special discount when ordered in
bulk quantities. Contact Prentice-Hall, Inc., General
Publishing Divison, Special Sales, Englewood Cliffs, N.J. 07632.

Prentice-Hall International, Inc., *London*
Prentice-Hall of Australia Pty. Limited, *Sydney*
Prentice-Hall Canada Inc., *Toronto*
Prentice-Hall of India Private Limited, *New Delhi*
Prentice-Hall of Japan, Inc., *Tokyo*
Prentice-Hall of Southeast Asia Pte. Ltd., *Singapore*
Whitehall Books Limited, *Wellington, New Zealand*
Editora Prentice-Hall do Brasil Ltda., *Rio de Janeiro*

Contents

for Robert Moody

Preface

This book is a systematic approach to painting theatrical scenery. It describes the techniques and tools that have been developed for or adapted to scene painting, the paints, and their use.

First the tools are discussed: what they are, what they are for, where to get them, and if need be, how they can be built. Paints and binders are discussed, and recipes for preparing them are provided.

Next the basic techniques that are the building blocks of scene painting are treated. The uses of each tool to get several effects are covered, as well as painting real objects, and the use of dopes and foams.

Combining the basic techniques to create a visually unified setting is the final step. The choice of color, technique, toning, and the like provides the scenery in each production with its own distinct character.

A complete glossary provides simple explanations of terms and concepts used in the paint shop.

Outside the professional shops, scene painting is an often neglected adjunct to scenic construction. Many times a well-designed and well-built set remains undistinguished because the painting is too flat, the colors contrast too much, or any number of other problems. Good scene painting can transform such scenery from mere acting space to an appropriate and visually pleasing dramatic environment.

This book outlines some methods and suggests an approach to painting scenery. It covers the basics and offers practical advice about choosing the right tools for the right tasks, the type of paint to use, and the appropriate techniques. It has a section on the application of color theory and a section covering the recipes for mixing the paints.

There is no pat color-by-number method for painting scenery. The scene painter must develop an eye for which techniques work where and learn to approach each project on its own terms, adapting the basic skills to each individual project. Mastery of the techniques is important, but the way they are put together by the scene painter determines how well the overall look of the scenery will work. The scenic designer has every reason to expect that his or her scenery will not only be blown up to full scale but that the character and style of the design will be preserved in the process. *Scene Painting* will help you develop an approach to using the techniques with style.

Program acknowledgments go to Lori Willis for helping with the preparation of the pictured examples, to Bob Moody and Harry Feiner for their encouragement and contributions, to Kate Soehlen for help pondering over the manuscript, and to Joseph Gilg for building sets well from incomplete plans while this book was in the works.

1 Introduction to the craft

SCENE PAINTING FOR THE THEATRE

Since the time of the ancient Greeks, scene painting has played a role in the theatre. Flats and drops have existed in some form since Roman times. Over the centuries scene painting has been an important element in scenic representation, although the responsibility for the painting has shifted among artists, architects, and scenic artists.

Sophocles created *skenographia*, or scene painting, nearly twenty-five centuries ago. Pollux reports that scenery was represented on tapestries and removable painted panels that were attached to *periaktoi*. These were three-sided structures with a triangular plan. The scenes were changed by revolving the panels to display another side. Scenic representations were painted on them, as well as symbols of gods that were used to accompany their entrances in the dramas.

There were two types of painted scenery in the Roman theatre. The first was a shiftable screen, similar to a modern flat. The other was a variation on the Greek periaktoi that involved a double-sided flat-like device that pivoted to display the scene painted on the back.

When theatre moved indoors after the outdoor performances of the Middle Ages, the stage space was reduced. This may have motivated the introduction of perspective scenery in the theatre. The use of perspective in scene painting made the scenes on stage appear larger, thus suggesting real-life scale.

Scene painting reached its peak during the Renaissance, when Italy revived scene painting and became the leader in scenic invention. Artists and architects there devised the scenery and experimented with composition and perspective. Shadows were painted on the same side of everything in a scene to suggest a single light source (even though the actual stage light usually came from a different angle). The perspective repre-

1

FIGURE 1–1. The Impresario.
Boston Conservatory of Music.
Designer and scene painter:
Harry Feiner.

sentation of architecture was very detailed and sophisticated. The convention was to use flat scenery that was painted to look extremely three-dimensional. The edges of these set pieces were cut out to enhance the perspective painted on them. Street scenes, for example, were painted on rows of cut-out wing flats so that it appeared as if the viewer were looking down a very long street. Borders were also cut out and painted in false perspective.

During the Baroque period the style used in scene painting was very similar to that used in mural or fresco painting. Painting with light and shade tones suggested motivated light sources. Scene painters were skilled craftsmen capable of painting full-size operatic scenery from the sketches of the designers, which weren't drawn to scale. This style of painting continued through the Romantic period and into the nineteenth century, when scenic art began a decline. Each theatre collected a stock of scenes, which were used over and over, mixed and matched in many different plays. In the late eighteenth century in England David Garrick employed Philippe DeLoutherbourg to try to reverse this kind of mediocrity in scenic spectacle. One of DeLoutherbourg's major contributions was to restore unity of design to scenery by personally overseeing all aspects of its creation.

At this time scenery was painted from cardboard models made by the designers. Sometimes the functions of the scene painter and the designer were merged in one individual. The painting of new scenes, including wings, borders, and drops, was done in a loft above the theatre.

In the early nineteenth century William Capon, who designed and painted at the Drury Lane Theatre, began to advocate architectural accuracy in scenery. This, along with DeLoutherbourg's scenic unity began a trend back toward the sophisticated scenery of the Renaissance, although that height has never again been reached in scene painting history.

Each theatre maintained a stock of pastoral scenes, castle interiors, and so on that were pulled from stock as needed. When the scenic artist decided to create a new scene, the event was advertised on handbills. These sets attracted audiences, who would sometimes go to view a favorite scene, or go to see a new scene unveiled.

Near the end of the nineteenth century, scene painting began to move out of the theatres and into scenic studios. The sets were built by carpenters from measured drawings provided by the designer, after which they were sent out to a scenic studio to be painted.

With the advent of realism and the introduction of the box set, new techniques were developed. Scenery became a

FIGURE 1–2. A vaudeville drop. These drops were used behind comedy and singing acts. Merchants could buy advertising space on them. *Used by permission of Charlotte's Web Music Cafe.*

FIGURE 1–3. Riverboat drop. Six Flags. *Scene painter: Robert Moody; Designer: Grady Larkins.*

FIGURE 1–4. Can-Can.
Boston Conservatory of Music.
Scene painter: Robert Moody;
Designer: Harry Feiner.

FIGURE 1–5. The Family. University of Missouri at
Kansas City. *Designer and scene painter: Harry Feiner.*

FIGURE 1–6. Uncle Vanya (drop for first scene).
Brandeis University. *Scene painter: Robert Moody;*
Designer: Melinda Leeson.

three-dimensional environment rather than the flat backing (or set of backings) it had been before. Where previously the painting had to define the set's form, the actual set pieces now took over that function. The concerns of the scene painter changed. Flats and other scenic elements were joined to make realistic forms, and it became the function of the painting to make the elements of scenery appear to be real wood, marble, wallpaper, stone, or any other material that was required.

Paint also has seen a renaissance as newer and, in some cases, better paints have been developed for theatrical use. Well into this century pigment still had to be mixed with size before painting could begin. Modern chemistry has devised new binders, and several good premixed paints have been developed for theatrical use.

Today the theatre has a creative hierarchy for producing plays. This hierarchy is strictly adhered to in the professional theatre to conform to the rules of the various unions. Other theatres use some variation of it depending on their individual situation and budget. It is not uncommon, for example, for the scenic designer also to fill the role of scene painter. Scene painting is only one aspect of a multifaceted collaboration. The entire production is co-ordinated by the play's director and the other members of the production staff.

The *production concept* is formulated by the director. It is a notion of what this production of the script will say, and how the production will go about saying it. It evolves with the participation of the production staff. A bare bones production staff consists of the director and the designers (scenic, costume, and

FIGURE 1–7. *Pippin* ("War").
· Rockford College Summer Theatre.
Designer and scene painter: Daniel Veaner.

FIGURE 1–8. *Pippin* ("The Flesh").
Rockford College Summer Theatre.
Designer and scene painter: Daniel Veaner.

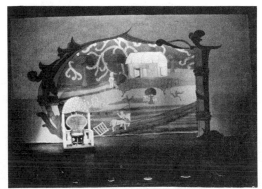

FIGURE 1–9. Oriental-style landscape. *Designer and Scene painter: Robert Moody.*

lighting). Other participants might be a choreographer, musical director, sound designer, and so on. The scenic designer works from the script, research, and the director's concept to create his design. This is articulated in the form of *renderings, sketches* (or *models*), and a *ground plan* to help the director visualize the proposed settings. Once the director has approved a final design the designer must rearticulate the design for the various technical crews whose job it is to translate the design into finished scenery.

Ground plans, sectionals, elevations, and detail drawings are drafted in scale for the carpentry crew. A set of detailed drawings goes to the props crew. The paint crew receives painter's elevations.

An elevation is a scaled front view of each piece of scenery. *Painter's elevations* are drawn in one-half-inch scale or in one-inch scale, usually on illustration board. The designer paints the elevations exactly the way he or she wants the scenery to look under work light (the lighting conditions under which the scenic artists will work). Color swatches are often provided so the scene painters can match the designer's palette, and notes on specific effects, techniques, or material specifications are also included.

The designer hands the proper documents to the appropriate crew head, and maintains a dialogue with each of them during the production process to make sure that the design is being executed as intended, and to keep design changes up to date. The hierarchy of technicians and craftspeople who work on the scenery is as follows:

FIGURE 1–10. Rendering. The scenery is portrayed as it will look under performance conditions: light, airy, theatrical.

FIGURE 1–11. Painter's elevation

FIGURE 1–12. Painter's elevation

What follows is the basic breakdown of individuals in a shop. Each situation has its own variation of the hierarchy based on this arrangement. In professional paint shops the hierarchy moves, in descending order of painting skill, from charge man down through detail men, layout men, lay-in men, and finally, paint boy.

As the modern theatre hierarchy has evolved, the responsibilities of the designer and scene painter have split. The designer is the one responsible for creating an appropriate dramatic environment that enhances both practical and artistic values of a production. Scene painting has evolved into one of the crafts that supports the work of the designer. A good scene painter should have an understanding of fine art and stage design, but no longer makes artistic decisions about a production.

The *charge man* is an essential figure in this hierarchy, the link between the designer and the rest of the crew. This is the one individual on the paint crew who must have a complete understanding of the designer's wishes so that the efforts of the whole group are coordinated to produce the correct, visually unified result. The charge man's judgment and visual sense reign over the other scene painters. Thus, the charge man must be a master scene painter who is familiar with every aspect of scene painting from bucket washing to the finest detail work.

Before starting it is a good idea for the charge man to take some time to explain the entire project to the crew. This practice builds morale and helps to insure visual unity because it gives each member of the paint crew the same idea of what the finished set should look like. As each painter works on a part of the set he or she can picture how that part fits into the whole, and work toward the same end as everyone else.

The charge man should have a chance to see the renderings during his or her initial conferences with the scenic designer. Renderings are paintings of the set as it will look under performance conditions. They are painted to look as if they are under stage lights, and a proportioned figure in costume is shown to give a sense of scale to the whole scene. From these the charge man can get an idea of the painting style the design-

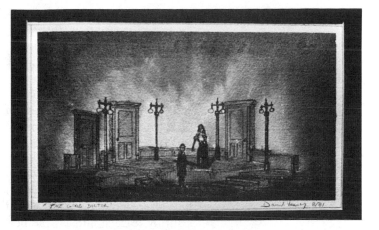

FIGURE 1–13. Rendering. The rendering is used to sell the scenic idea to the director.

FIGURE 1–14. After the set has been approved, it should end up looking very close to the rendering.

er is using. At the first crew call it is also useful to show the renderings to the other scene painters if they are available.

The charge man assigns tasks to each member of the crew and oversees the painting of the set. While this is going on he or she communicates with the designer, who may suggest changes or clarify aspects of the design.

All the scene painting is done from the painter's elevations, except occasionally when it is done from a scale model of the set. Scaled scenic models, like painter's elevations, are painted as the set would look under work light. They are usually constructed in one-half-inch scale. Colors are mixed and matched against the colors on the elevations. The painting techniques the designer wants used are indicated on the elevations as a guide for the scene painters.

Scene painting may seem less important today than it was

in the Romantic period or in the Renaissance. It is true that a lot of techniques from those periods have been lost. A production's dependence upon scenery, especially painted scenery, has diminished considerably in the last century-and-a-half. But in some ways scene painting has become more important, because modern designers use so many different styles. The modern scene painter must be prepared to paint anything from the simplest wood technique to a complicated city scene. This current state of affairs has made the role of the scene painter more difficult in some ways, but definitely more exciting. Each new set requires a unique approach that makes new demands on the painting. The scene painter does not simply crank out the same type of scenery show after show. One show may have an excruciatingly realistic interior, the next may take a constructivist approach, the next a multi-drop romantic look, and so on. The scene painter must be capable of approaching each production as a new problem to be solved.

For every new show a fresh approach to the scene painting must be developed. Such an approach uses the same basic scene painting techniques in unique ways that are appropriate to the individual style of the scene design. A scene painter skilled in the basics should be able to approach any set that may be assigned and figure out the best way to paint it so it retains the stylistic character that the designer has specified in the renderings and elevations. Each project must be begun with an open mind, and the scene painter's knowledge of the basics should be built upon to construct a comprehensive approach to the individual show. In this way a modern scene painter can be versatile enough to paint any show that comes along, and to infuse a spirit of innovation and growth into the execution of each scenic design.

FIGURE 1–15. Elevation. Elevations of drops are painted to scale.

FIGURE 1–16. Painter's elevation.
A set piece is painted to scale on illustration
board as it should look under work light.

FIGURE 1–17. Finished set piece

SCENE PAINTING AS A CRAFT

Scene painting as a craft is very much alive. The scene painter shares many skills with the fine artist, but in the current theatre hierarchy it is the scenic designer who makes artistic decisions. The scene painter may be likened to a craftsperson who casts a sculptor's work. The charge man is given a set of painter's elevations or a model from which the larger work will be cast. Instructions as to color, texture, and style are laid out in detail.

A master scene painter will create the desired result by dealing with the whole effect the designer intends to create. With his own special knowledge of the craft ways are found to reach the visual goals of the designer. The main clues the designer provides to his or her vision of the finished scenery are in the renderings of the set. A sense of mood and drama is infused into these sketches that the designer may not be able to articulate verbally. The scene painter must have some knowledge of stage design in order to interpret the renderings and the sketches meaningfully. The point of scene painting is to arrive at the designer's vision. An understanding of what goes on in a designer's mind, and an ability to portray it meaningfully in the painting of the scenery ultimately requires that the scene painter be a part of the collaboration that makes a set—and a show—work.

The renderings are a valuable resource for the scene painter when developing an overall approach to the painting style. Should the painting be tight and precise as it might be in a production of *Hedda Gabler,* or free flowing as it could be on a set for *The Madwoman of Chaillot?* Considerations of style are very important to the finished scenery, and should be worked out by the charge man before painting is begun.

One of the main considerations is the actual style of the painting. This involves more than simply choosing individual techniques. All of the tangible and intangible aspects of the visual style help to set the tone and mood of the play. The type and sweep of brush strokes, their textural qualities, color palette, and visual focus combine to produce an intangible quality to the scenic environment that the audience responds to on an emotional level. This quality must be integrated with the other aspects of the production, and it must be the result of the scene painter correctly representing the designer's work. This is why it is so important for the scene painter to have an opportunity to view the renderings, and to be in communication with the designer throughout the production period.

Another consideration is that the set should appear to have been painted by a single artist, while in reality it has been painted by several individuals. No matter how careful each one is to duplicate the techniques as determined by the charge man, every painter's style is slightly different. Some scene painters are stronger in some areas of painting than others. There must be a harmonious melding of these individual styles to avoid an uneven patchwork of techniques.

It is up to the charge man to see to it that the work of all the scene painters on the crew is blended into a unified whole. One method is to assign the scene painters tasks that best fit their talents. A scene painter who is particularly good at painting foliage is assigned all the leaves, one who's strength lies in painting clouds puts in the sky, and so on. This ensures that each aspect of the painting is consistent within itself. Then the various parts of the scene must be blended so they result in a unified whole. This is done in part by choosing the techniques to be used and, finally, by bringing them together using blending and toning.

Another approach to creating visual unity from several scene painters' styles works equally well. All of the scene painters on the crew paint everything in a scene, but they frequently change places so that no one area of the set is the work of a single person. This mixes up the individual styles so that they merge into a single look.

Ultimately the charge man must take the responsibility for the look of the painting. No matter how skilled the individuals on the crew are it is essential that one person be in charge, making all the decisions on style and technique. Painting by committee runs the real risk of watering down the techniques to suit everybody until there is no sense of style left at all. The charge man's main mission is to influence the painting style so that it is visually unified, unique, and a sensitive translation of the scene design.

The size of the scenery and of the theatre are also factors in the consideration of style. In a house with a ninety-foot proscenium that seats thousands of spectators an extremely broad style of painting is used. Small detail painting won't read beyond the third row. Smaller, more intimate theatres require more precise, careful work, even when a broad effect is wanted. Scenery painted for a small theatre would look silly in a huge one, and vice versa.

It is important that the scenery be unified in technique as well as style. This means that when the individual techniques are chosen they will work well together to create the look that is wanted. In addition, all the painting of a particular technique on a set should be consistent with all the other painting of that particular technique. Consistency in the painting goes a long way toward tying together the look of a scene.

The final result of the scene painting should be visually

unified and consistent with the designer's vision. Moreover, it should be consistent with all the other aspects of the production. It is true that it is the responsibility of the production staff to coordinate their areas of influence, but that does not let any of the artists or craftspeople off the hook. The more the charge man communicates with the scenic designer and with the paint crew, the more likely the work is to be consistent with what all the designers, the director, and the actors are doing.

Scale

Since it's very difficult, if not impossible, to view the scenery in its entirety while working on it in the paint shop, it is important that the scene painter develop a refined sense of scale. It is always important to back up frequently to look at the scenery from the same distance at which the audience will view it. If the scene painter retreats about fifteen feet from the work in progress and squints slightly the scenery will appear close to how it will look on stage. Proportion and techniques must be checked constantly in this way. Often it will be found that what seems close up like a perfectly good curve will appear kinked and uneven from a distance. With experience the individual will learn to gauge how scene painting reads to the audience, but frequent double checking is the only way to be sure.

Obviously, the reason painter's elevations are scaled is so the scene painter can measure the drawing onto the scenery. It is worth taking the time to do this carefully. Once the essential drawing has been measured on, it can be corrected by stepping back to check proportions and consistency of line against the elevation.

One problem many beginning scene painters have with large scale is controlling the brush. In small-scale sketching usually the pencil is held between the fingers and controlled from the wrist. In scene painting the whole body must be used in order to get the leverage needed to paint so large. Novices worry that it is difficult to work precisely on scenery painted on the floor with brush extenders. The brush, whether it is on an extender or not, must not be treated as a separate tool. It must become an extension of the body and, as such, it will be easier to control it while painting.

Plan of Attack

Even more than waiting for a kettle to boil, watching paint dry ranks among the world's most fruitless activities. Given that most theatrical shops constantly work under monstrous deadlines it can be an expensive waste of time. A good scene painter will come to the shop prepared with a rough schedule for the day as well as an overall plan for the whole project. Not only is the crew's time valuable, but often the time allotted for using the shop space for painting does not allow time for large pieces of scenery to lie fallow.

The charge man should work out a plan of attack, and try to keep the crew as close to this schedule as possible. Extra time should be built in to accommodate unexpected additions by the designer, or for setbacks in the work. Jobs should be staggered so that when one piece of scenery cannot be worked on another task will be waiting to fill in that unexpected free time. While a size coat or base coat dries, numerous other jobs can continue. Paint can be mixed and tested for the next phase of the project, or work on other projects can go forward. The time the drop takes to dry provides an opportunity to paint the furniture, mouldings, or smaller set pieces. Also, coffee or lunch breaks for the crew should be fit logically into this plan. If a drop is base coated just before lunch it will be dry when the crew returns to work.

Certain tasks should be performed late in the day to prepare for the next morning such as laying out and sizing a drop. The next morning the crew can begin right away on another phase of the painting. In shops that use pigment paints the pastes for the next day should be prepared in the late afternoon. This allows the pigment to become saturated with size overnight to form more consistent paint, as well as providing the benefit of not having to wait in the morning for the paint to be prepared. Some amount of cleaning and maintenance at the end of the day can make the next day's work go more smoothly. Finally, the preparation of special tools such as stencils or pounces can save hours of waiting the next day.

In a professional shop good organization is essential because it can save a considerable sum of money in wages, but in any shop it can save on physical and human resources. There is certainly no shame in finishing the scenery on time, or even (gasp!) early. The syndrome of painting Act 2 during Act 1 on opening night can and should be avoided by planning the shop time well.

Planning Work Space

By taking a moment to plan the use of the work space a lot of time can be saved. When laying out a drop on the floor, for example, there should be space around each side to allow enough room for walking around the drop and placing paint and equipment around it. This will save the crew having to balance precariously around the work.

Space should be allowed for scene painters to back up to view the scenery as it is painted, an important part of the scene painting process. If enough space is not allowed the scene painter's effectiveness is crippled. Some sort of ladder, scaffold, or catwalk should be available to view scenery that is painted on the floor.

Finally, pieces of scenery should be arranged for painting in a logical order, according to their position when assembled on stage. In a box set the walls are numbered in order on the elevations and ground plan, and the actual scenic units should be set up in that order so that wallpaper and other similar effects will match up at the corners. All sets have some order to them, even if they are not comprised of realistic walls. It is useful, as well as time saving, to paint them according to their own particular logic. If there is some doubt as to which piece is which, the carpenters should be prevailed upon to label each piece with a number or letter that is consistent with a similar label on the ground plan. This practice insures that when the set is assembled the painting will make sense.

Light

Painter's elevations are rendered as if the set pieces were under work light when painted. It is therefore useful to define what work light is. Most shops have areas where the painting is most often done, even if there is not a proper paint shop in the facility. It is helpful to set up a permanent set of work lights for painting. Scoops make very good work lights, because they are stage lighting instruments, and will simulate the intensity and general quality of light used on stage. Of course, no color filters should be put in these lights in the shop.

In areas where the scenery is usually painted up the scoops should be hung at an angle that evenly distributes the light without casting the scene painter's shadow onto the work. Two or more scoops separated by at least six feet will go a long way toward relieving the problem of shadows. An angle of about thirty degrees from the paint frame wall is sharp enough to reduce the difficulty with shadows yet shallow enough not to distort the reflection of the light off the scenery. Scoops should be hung around the floor area where large scenery, such as drops, are painted. If they are angled from two different directions, shadows will not be a problem. It is also useful to have one or two booms on wheeled stands with scoops on them for working in odd areas of the shop or on stage.

It is important that there be enough light in the paint area. Stage lighting tends to be very bright, and dim shop light will not show the work under the same conditions it will be seen in the theatre.

Mixing Enough Paint

There may be nothing more frustrating for a scene painter than to run out of base coat color with only three square feet of scenery left to paint. Unfortunately there is no magic formula for figuring out the right amount of paint to the ounce, but with experience the scene painter will learn how to make fairly accurate estimates. The thickness of the paint, the absorbency of the scenic material, and the individual technique of the scene painter are all factors that affect the volume of paint needed.

It is always best to mix a bit more paint than is needed. Even when you are confined to a limited budget it is better to overestimate so that the scene painter will be assured of enough paint to finish the scenery. Matching a new batch of color to an old one is difficult and time consuming. The extra paint usually gets used for something, and if there is too much left it can always be mixed into another color that is needed.

Testing Colors

It is rare for a show to be painted just with factory-mixed colors out of the can. But under any circumstances the colors should be tested on a test flat that is covered with a surface material matching the scenery surfaces. Perception of a color is effected by the colors that surround it. The same purple will seem redder next to blue, and bluer next to red. Therefore, it is important that the scene painter see all the colors in the relationship they will have when painted onto the scenery. It is much better to do this on a small test area than to discover the relationships are all wrong on the larger scenery.

Another reason the colors must be tested is that scene paint does not dry the same color it looks when it is wet. Most colors dry a shade or two lighter, depending on the type of paint, and if there is white mixed into it the color dries several shades lighter. This makes it particularly important to test the paint, allowing the test splotches to completely dry before considering the color adjustment finished.

Preparing to paint is often tiresome, and can be at least as time consuming as the painting itself. However, proper preparation will pay off in the long run in time, money, and the advantage of painting under optimum conditions.

Ordering Supplies

Ordering supplies and paint usually fall under the jurisdiction of the charge man or shop head. Brushes, tools, glues, equipment, and, of course, paint are all in this category. There are two different circumstances the shop head may find himself or herself in: ordering for a single show, or stocking a shop for a whole season.

It is probably more difficult to order materials for a single show. Estimates of materials needed must be quite accurate. It is usually wise to buy locally, so if a color runs out it can be replenished quickly, and extra supplies can be returned. This can limit the type of paint that can be used to whatever is in stock at the local hardware or paint store.

The shop head should have all the elevations and plans

when estimating how much of which colors are going to be needed. In a case like this it is wise to over-order by a quarter to a third. Most people tend to underestimate, especially when trying to stay under budget, and wishful thinking usually results in running out of supplies too soon. Over-ordering insures that there will be enough paint to finish the set, allowing for unforeseen problems and at least one touch-up after the set has been assembled in the theatre.

Stocking a shop for a longer season is a bit less pressure laden, but it poses its own peculiar problems. Usually the show titles for a season are announced ahead of time, but the designs are rarely ready for all the shows in advance of the season. The shop head has to guess what the scenery will be like or wait to stock for that show. There are considerable savings to be gained when buying in bulk, and often it is necessary to just go ahead and guess. The designers should be consulted, because even if the designs are not on paper yet they may have some idea of what their sets will be like. If the season leans toward shows with a lot of exterior scenes, the shop should have extra volumes of earth colors on hand. There are enough clues to roughly estimate what will be needed. It is impossible to be completely accurate, but certain titles suggest certain color ranges. About a third of the paint budget should be left unencumbered to allow for stock and adjustments and incidental purchases.

The individual who stocks the shop should keep a running inventory of paint and materials. Lists should be kept of quantities used for each show, and charged accordingly. Soon he or she will be better able to estimate inventory for future shows and seasons using the hard facts of past experience.

By keeping track of what is needed and what is used a shop can remain well-stocked from year to year. Budget planning is facilitated, and it is even possible to acquire some overstock by building upon past years' purchases. The stock of capital equipment such as brushes and other nonexpendable tools can also be built up gradually over a period of years. A shop should not be stocked beyond its storage capacity, however. Pigments and dry glues should have adequate dry storage space, and canned paints need to be stored within prescribed environmental limitations. Premixed paints tend to settle in the can, so if a lot of them are stocked over a long period of time there should be some facility provided for keeping them mixed up.

With careful management the stock of brushes and tools in the shop can be increased, as well as the stock of expendable materials. Buckets seem to be the most expended "nonexpendable" item. Plastic buckets are the lesser of the available evils in that they are reusable, and relatively easy to clean. One must be careful to buy the type that are made of flexible plastic, because the brittle plastic buckets tend to crack and break. Five-quart and five-gallon buckets are the most useful sizes. Small plastic freezer containers with tight lids are excellent for keeping small amounts of paint and metallics and are inexpensively obtained.

The shop should have a good selection of different types and sizes of brushes. It should contain its own set of tools separate from the carpenters' tools, so that paint work is never held up by attempts to track down a hammer or staple gun.

As much as possible paint and equipment should be ordered locally for convenience. When buying a lot of paint, however, the shop head should call around and comparison shop. Sometimes a better deal can be found out of town because of lower prices or professional discounts that are not available locally, even when shipping charges are added in. In such cases the shop head should obtain assurances of the availability of the materials, and try to ascertain the shipping date. This precaution will avoid unexpected backorders that could hold up the painting indefinitely. Naturally, this sort of purchasing should take place well before the season begins.

2 Tools and the paint shop

Each theatre has a different arrangement of scene painting space. Many professional shops and theatres have a separate paint shop. Often the painting area is shared with the carpentry shop. In some educational and community theatres the stage itself is the painting space. The location and set-up of the painting space greatly effects the scene painter's ability to work quickly and efficiently. Heat, humidity, accessibility to a sink and other equipment, integrity of the painting areas (floors, frames, and so on) are all factors that determine how good a space is.

The most desirable location for the paint shop is near the construction shop, with easy access between the two. When shop space is shared some tactical ingenuity is needed, because the construction and paint crews compete for the same work space. Unwanted effects might result from sawdust or other particles mixing into the paint.

There should be plenty of space for laying out full-stage-sized scenery in the paint shop. There should also be ample space for storing equipment and paint, mixing colors and storing scenery. The painting and mixing areas should be well lit, and tool storage areas should be easily accessible to the work areas.

The well-equipped paint shop should contain certain essential areas and equipment, including the work space itself, a utility sink, stove, palette tables, storage and mixing cabinets, and a size barrel.

Work Space

Scenery is *painted up* in an upright position, or *down* on the floor. Each presents advantages and disadvantages. Painting up can be more convenient in many instances. The scene painter can paint without constantly stooping and kneeling to reach the scenery, which greatly relieves back and neck strain. It is consid-

FIGURE 2–1. A paint shop with storage and mixing areas, sink, stove, and painting areas.

erably easier to step back to view the work in progress when painting up. Finally, the paint buckets are on the same level with the painter and with the area of scenery that is being worked on. Without a motorized paint frame, however, access to tall scenery is difficult, and paint tends to run and drip if it is too generously applied.

The opposite considerations apply to painting down. Even when brush extenders are used there is a great deal of bending needed. The buckets are on the floor and must be carried around. In order to view the scenery to check for proportion and continuity of line the painter must climb a ladder or scaffold, which provides a somewhat distorted view, not to mention a precarious perch. On the positive side, the paint does not drip, and the floor provides a hard, consistent backing, particularly useful for drops and scrim. If a puddling technique is wanted it can only be done on the floor. By the same token, if puddling is not wanted the scene painter has to be careful to avoid doing it by mistake.

A floor used for a painting area should be a smooth, wooden floor, at least the size of a full stage drop. Concrete floors will not take nails or staples, so there is no way to tack a drop down or nail into it for line snapping. Many shop floors are difficult to work on because they have electrical outlets built into them and these will show up on a drop just as a penny under a piece of paper shows up when rubbed over with a pencil.

The floor should be kept in good condition. Any nails or staples should be carefully removed after each project. Noncolorfast dyes and paints should be carefully mopped up so they will not soak through future scenery projects. Splintered or dented areas should be repaired, because they will show up in a drop.

FIGURE 2–2.
A motorized paint frame

In larger theatres imperfections in the painting caused by the floor surface will not read, but a damaged floor starts each project with a handicap, so it is worthwhile to care for it.

When a paint frame is used it should be at least as large as a full stage drop. The frame, like the floor, should be kept free of nails, staples and noncolorfast paints and dyes. The trough on the bottom of the frame should be kept clean of dirt, sawdust, paint, foam chips or other materials that may be picked up by a wet brush and inadvertently mixed into the paint. The floor in front of the frame should also be kept clean with frequent sweeping and mopping.

Sink A good sized utility sink is one of the most essential items in the paint shop. It should have hot and cold water, and it is useful to add a screen or filter to prevent the drain from getting clogged with paint. Most paint used for scenery mixes and cleans up with water, so easy access is particularly important. Counters and brush storage cabinets should be located within reach of the sink for easy access when cleaning buckets or brushes, as well as for paint mixing. A five-gallon bucket or a four-gallon pump sprayer tank should fit under the faucet, and be easily removed after being filled with water. A movable faucet makes it easier to handle large containers in the sink. It is also useful for a hose fitting to be attached to the faucet.

Storage and Work Surfaces When planning storage areas the characteristics of the materials to be stored must be taken into consideration. Pigment, analine dyes, and powdered charcoal must be stored in a dry environ-

FIGURE 2–3.
Storage and mixing table.
Has ample mixing surface with
easy access to color.

ment. Premixed paints and pastes can be adversely affected by extreme temperatures. It is also important that paint storage be reasonably near the mixing area, and that the mixing area be close to the sink.

Perhaps one of the more successful types of cabinet variations is a combination storage and mixing table. The lower part is a large cabinet with doors on each side for storage of gallon cans of paint. This is topped by a counter top for color mixing. One or two shelves are built above the counter to store a can of each color in current use. Under the lower shelf a light is installed to help see color while mixing, and on the side of the cabinet a rack is built to hold yard sticks, brush extenders and other long tools. The whole unit is built on casters, which is especially convenient when shop space is limited. Other combinations of cabinets, lockers, counters and so on are equally acceptable, but they should have the following qualities: adequate, secure storage space for the usual amount of paint stored in the shop, and ample, well-lit counter space for color mixing.

If a lot of paint or paste is being stored over a long period of time the shop should stock one or more mixing devices, because the heavier pigment and binder in paint tends to settle, separating from the lighter water. Paint that has been sitting on the shelf for a long period of time needs to be stirred before it settles into an irretrievable hardened mass. The best solution to this difficulty is a paint-shaking device such as those used in paint stores. This will thoroughly shake up one or two cans at a time without having to open the cans and exposing the paint to the air. Another solution is to use a mixer device that attaches to an electric drill. These come in several sizes. They consist of a kind of propeller on the end of a shaft, which fits into the drill chuck. If neither of these devices is available, the paint will require more frequent care. Cans should be opened periodically and stirred with a long, flat mixing stick. It also helps to turn the paint cans over every so often to reverse the direction that the paint settles in.

A pigment palette cabinet is used to store dry pigment, dry glues, whiting, or other powdered substances. This is usually a wooden cabinet with bins built into it for each color, in ascending rows for easy access. This cabinet should also be built on wheels. Pigment usually comes from the supplier in paper bags, which are then dumped into the appropriately labeled bin in the cabinet. These cabinets are built with a lid to cover the bins and, thus, protect the powders. If a large volume of pigment is stocked, a less compact storage arrangement is used. A wooden rack is constructed, supported against a wall, on which rows of five-gallon buckets with tight lids are fitted. (These

FIGURE 2–4. Pigment and palette cabinet. Used for storing dry pigments and powders.

FIGURE 2–5. Pigment rack. Used to store large volumes of pigment.

FIGURE 2–6. Brush cabinet. Large brushes hang from their handles, liners are stored upside down in bins. Drainage is below.

buckets come in plastic, as for packaging cleaning chemicals, or in heavy cardboard, as for ice cream parlour bins). Each lid is labeled with the contents of the bucket. Containers this size hold more than enough pigment for the average shop stock.

Since brushes are usually stored while still drying, brush cabinets should be built to facilitate this. The best position for a drying paint brush is hanging from its handle with the bristles down. This allows excess water to drip out of the bristles without bending them, or soaking the glue that holds them onto the brush. If it's impossible to fit all the brushes into such an arrangement the second best choice is to prop the brushes upside down, being careful the bristles are not leaning against anything. It is important to keep this in mind when designing a brush storage cabinet, because scene painting brushes are useless if the bristles are not kept straight. The brush cabinet should contain hooks or finishing nails from which to hang brushes by the hole on the end of their handles. If there is not space to store all the brushes this way, liners especially lend themselves to being stored bristle side up in bins built into the bottom of the cabinet. Water dripping out of freshly cleaned brushes needs someplace to go to avoid mildewing. If window screen vents are built into the bottom of the cabinet, drainage and ventilation are adequately provided for. A well-designed brush cabinet is placed over the sink so that drainage is provided for. In most shops it is important that the brush storage cabinet can be locked. Paint brushes are frequently grabbed by unthinking individuals who need a glue brush, and who invariably leave the brush in the glue until it has become fossilized. Because this unmalicious, but nonetheless prevalent, syndrome is a reality of shop life, it is

useful to store several inexpensive brushes prominently in an open cabinet well removed from the scene painting brushes.

Other equipment should also have secure storage space provided. Cabinet space should be provided for all the odd tools for pouncing, stapling, and so on. Sponges and other tools for applying paint should be stored in ventilated cabinets like brushes are. Special metal cabinets are manufactured for storing spray paint and toxic or flammable supplies. Racks should be provided for straight edges, stamps, stencils, drawing sticks, and other such tools.

Finally, the paint shop should have its own small stock of shop tools, securely stored near the painting areas. This should include staple guns and a one-hundred-foot tape measure for tacking down drops, screwdrivers or other tools for pulling out staples, one or two hammers and a small supply of duplex nails for fastening scenery to the paint frame, an electric drill for mixing paint, an adjustable crescent wrench for repairing pump sprayers, putty knives, scissors, X-acto®or mat knives for stencil cutting, and a hot melt glue gun.

Palette Tables

A palette table is a very useful piece of equipment. It is a long, thin table, about thirty inches high, mounted on casters. Sometimes it has a lower shelf. Once the paint has been mixed, all the appropriate buckets for a particular job are placed on the palette table, and wheeled to the work area. The scene painters can roll the palette for a piece of scenery along with them as they go, reducing travelling time from scenery to bucket. Although it may seem like a small point, the less time spent walking back and forth between the scenery and paint buckets, the more can be spent actually painting, which is, after all, the main order of business. In theatres with their own paint shops attached, paint is also wheeled on stage for touch-ups on palette tables.

FIGURE 2–7. Palette table allows palette and equipment to be wheeled to the work.

**Glue Pot
and Stove**

The paint shop should contain a stove or heavy duty hot plate and a modest selection of pots and pans for mixing glue, dye, starch, dope, and so on, not to mention coffee for the crew. A double boiler is essential, especially for breaking down any of the binders that come in powdered or crystal form. As these glues tend to smell pretty badly after a short time, it is worthwhile to keep these utensils reasonably clean. When large volumes of water need to be heated, as for mixing starch, metal pails make good pots.

Commercial electric glue pots are available from some theatrical supply companies. These are similar to "crock pots," and have the heating attributes of a double boiler. It is still useful to stock a stove for other applications that require larger or different containers.

FIGURE 2–8. A typical stove and glue pot with a paint shaker for reviving shelf stock.

Size Barrel

The size barrel is usually a large plastic trash barrel with a lid. Shops that primarily use pigment paint need a size barrel because paint is not only broken down with size, but is thinned with it instead of water. Even shops that use premixed paints might use a size barrel if there is a large volume of fabric scenery to be primed. Alongside the barrel a 1-by-3 board about four feet long should be kept handy for stirring.

The most frequent difficulty with the size barrel is that it is mistaken for a trash can. Even a large, red sign on the lid is often insufficient to keep refuse out of the size. Storing the size barrel out of the line of traffic, occasionally straining the size, and a sense of humor will minimize the problem considerably.

Access Equipment   The paint shop should contain some or all of the following items for painting scenery up: ladders, a scaffold, and a paint frame. The shop should be minimally equipped with a few A-ladders of different heights. A-ladders are usually equipped with a shelf near the top that folds out to hold paint buckets. The shelf is of limited use, because it only holds one bucket at a time, and the effective work area is limited by the scene painter's arm length. A lot of climbing up and down with buckets and equipment is required, wasting a lot of time and energy. Nevertheless, A-ladders can provide access to spaces where larger scaffolds will not fit.

Multileveled, wheeled scaffolds are useful for painting tall scenery propped against a wall, or fastened to an immobile paint frame. Several varieties of light-weight aluminum scaffolding on casters are available. Many of these are designed to break down into component parts for easy storage, and as many or as few levels as are needed can be assembled for each job. One or more scene painters and all their paint and equipment fit on the plank flooring of the scaffold. With the help of an assistant on the ground to push the scaffold along the scenery as it is painted, large set pieces can be finished quickly.

Paint frames are large wooden framed units, hung against a wall in the shop, onto which scenery is tacked for painting up. Some paint frames are fixed, but the most useful ones are movable. The unit is either counterweighted or motorized so that it can be lowered into a slot in the floor of the shop. This allows the scene painter to remain at ground level with all the paint and equipment while the scenery rises and descends to the desired level. If possible, scenery should not be fastened onto the lower two or three feet of the frame so that the scenic artist can paint the entire piece from a standing position, and to keep paint and other stuff that collects in the trough at the bottom of the frame from getting on the scenery.

Thin pieces of scenery can be painted on a paint frame. Cut-outs, drops, and flats are common examples. Some care must be exercised in fastening flats so that the bottoms do not catch on the edge of the slot (the frame will continue to descend, bending the caught flat until it smashes into smithereens). The scene painter should also expect to drop yard sticks, ink markers, elevations, and other things down the slot, and be resigned to travelling downstairs to retrieve them.

TOOLS   Most people who have worked in a carpentry shop have heard the expression, "use the right tool for the right job." This rule of thumb is equally appropriate in the scene painting shop. Learning to use the different tools correctly enables the scene painter to get more work done quickly and efficiently. In a job already beset by frantic deadlines it is important to make proper use of the tools so that more time can be spent where it should be—painting scenery.

Brushes

The brush is the most basic scenepainting tool. Though it is a simple device, it is worth taking the time to understand how it works. A brush is made up of three parts: the *handle*, the *ferrule*, and the *bristles*. A good brush has a handle that fits the painter's hand easily and comfortably. Some brushes come with a hole in the end of the handle so the brush can be hung up to dry. Such a hole is easily drilled if the handle does not come that way. The ferrule is a metal band that holds the bristles together and attaches them to the handle. The top end of the bundle of bristles is glued into the ferrule, which is tacked into the lower end of the handle. Brush bristles are either natural animal bristles or made of synthetic materials such as nylon. Finer quality brushes are made of boar bristles.

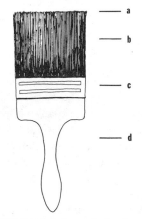

FIGURE 2–9. Parts of a brush: (a) flag; (b) bristles; (c) ferrule; (d) handle

If the budget allows it, natural bristle brushes should be used. Scene painting is similar in all but scale to watercoloring, and the softer natural bristles allow the paint to flow onto scenery with a more watercolor-like quality. Nylon brushes distribute the paint in harder, scratchy strokes, and don't hold the paint as well.

When the brush is dipped into the paint, the liquid clings to each individual bristle. In this manner a brush can hold a reasonable volume of paint. When applied to scenery the paint runs along the bristle to the end, which distributes the paint to the surface. Each bristle is *flagged* (split at the end), which further helps the brush to distribute the paint smoothly. The amount of pressure exerted on the brush, along with the amount of paint it is holding determines how much paint is administered to the scenery. With practice the scene painter can paint long, even lines by slowly increasing the pressure on the brush as its supply of paint runs out.

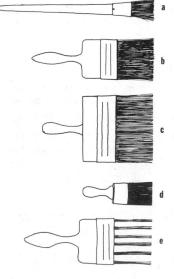

FIGURE 2–10. Types of scene painting brushes: (a) liner; (b) priming brush; (c) lay-in brush; (d) stencil brush; (e) finger brush

The bristles present anywhere between two and five usable surfaces, depending on how they are bunched and the shape of the ferrule. The normal brush stroke involves using the end of the brush, dragging the flag across the surface of the scenery. Different strokes and marks can be made using the sides, and this is done frequently, especially when painting foliage.

Several types of brush have been developed for use in painting scenery. Each has a specific purpose, and comes in a range of sizes. It is usually best to use the largest appropriate brush for each aspect of a project. Using a one-inch brush to paint a two-inch line doubles the time and effort needed for the job. When working on a large, varied project it is useful to have a selection of different sized brushes on hand.

Liners. A liner, as the name implies, is used for painting lines. It is a relatively small brush with a long handle. Small liners, also referred to as detail brushes, come in sizes between a quarter of an inch to an inch (although some even smaller sizes are available in some brands). A well-equipped shop will have a stock of these brushes in one-quarter-inch, one-half-inch, three-quarter-inch and one-inch sizes. Larger liners, known as foliage brushes, fitches, or decorating brushes are available in sizes up to three inches. These brushes are used for numerous texture techniques as well as for large lines and foliage painting.

Long liners have longer bristles which can hold more paint and are thus capable of painting longer, uninterrupted lines. *Round liners* and *flat liners* are brushes whose names refer to the shape of the ferrule, which dictates the shape of the bristle bundle. Round liners are used for lettering. Flat liners, with rectangular or oblong ferrules are the most often used type of liner.

The ends of liners are flat, not pointed like artist's watercolor brushes. This is so a one-half-inch liner, for example, will produce a one-half-inch line. The measurement refers to the width of the ferrule. The bristles come virtually straight out from the ferrule, producing a line of the same width. Fitch brushes have a trapezoidal ferrule from which the bristles taper out, producing a somewhat wider line.

Priming brushes. Priming brushes are used to cover large areas quickly. They are used for base coats, prime coats and size coats. They are quite large with ferrules that are six or seven inches wide and one to three inches thick.

Laying-in brushes. Laying-in brushes are middle-sized brushes used for painting in large, but not huge, areas of a scene. These brushes can be purchased in local hardware or paint stores, and are the typical brush most people picture when they think of a paint brush.

Stencil brushes. A stencil brush is a small, round-ferruled brush with a short handle. It is not used for making long brush strokes as other brushes are, but for twisting motions or stippling through a stencil.

Finger brushes. A finger brush is a specialty brush with several bristle bundles in a row. It can be used for effects such as coarse wood graining or crosshatching. Multiple ferruled finger brushes are available on the market, but the scene painter can simply achieve the same effect by giving a laying-in brush a haircut, creating spaces between bunches of bristles along the ferrule. Finger brushes are usually dragged across the scenery to create several thin, parallel lines.

Expendable Materials

There are several expendable materials that are often used for scene painting. The greatest of these are, of course, paints and glues. But there are several others that are used with almost equal frequency, if not volume. Generally, you discover that you have run out of these items just as you are ready to start working on a project, so it is almost essential to stock them in greater quantity than you anticipate.

Charcoal. Charcoal is used in two forms: stick (also called vine charcoal), and powdered. When buying charcoal sticks it is important to specify the soft kind that has no oily substance in it. Charcoal is usually used for roughing in drawings or gridding, and it must come off the scenery as easily as it goes on. Nonoily charcoal leaves a powder on the scenery that will cling sufficiently for this purpose without remaining when it is unwanted. Hard charcoal must be ground in harder to produce a line, making it harder to remove. The oil used in some charcoal acts as a binder. In both cases the charcoal is held on so well that the lines cannot be eliminated. This is especially bad when trying to get rid of a charcoal grid in a sky or other light area of a drop, or when trying to erase the guide lines for a wallpaper stencil.

The sticks come in several sizes. The thinnest size is too small for the purposes of scene painting. Since there is little to hold the charcoal in the form of a stick, the small ones disinte-

FIGURE 2–11. Charcoal stick, charcoal powder, chalk stick, chalk powder, ink marker, tape, staples

grate too fast. Medium-thick sticks should be used for drawing, gridding, and so forth. Fat sticks should be kept on hand to use with bow-type snap lines.

Powdered charcoal is used for pouncing. Some paint merchants will say that tempera works as well (especially if they do not have powdered charcoal and want to make a sale anyway), but it does not. Tempera goes on just fine, but is very difficult to get off. The powder that remains mixes with the paint that is brushed on, darkening the color, or streaking. Powdered charcoal can sometimes be found in art supply stores, or obtained from scene paint suppliers. It comes in tin cans that keep moisture out to prevent lumps from forming. In addition to pouncing, powdered charcoal can be put in a chalk line for snapping lines over large areas.

Chalk. Stick chalk is rarely used in the paint shop, but it is useful to have a few pieces lying around for marking points on the floor and other odd jobs. Powdered chalk is used in chalk lines to snap lines on the floor when laying down a drop. It should not be used on scenery, because it does not come off easily. It is available in hardware stores and comes in plastic squeeze bottles. These should be saved after the chalk is used up, because they are great for dispensing dope and white glue. Powdered chalk comes in a few colors, the most prevalent of which seems to be blue.

Ink markers. With the popularity of felt tip pens many different brands of ink marker have appeared on the market. Everyone has a favorite, but because most scene paint is water based ink markers used in the paint shop must contain waterproof ink. Water soluble inks run, fade, and cause other nasty problems. If there is some question as to whether the ink is waterproof, don't use it.

Brown is a good color for inking in a drawing. It is dark enough for the scene painter to see while working on a project, but light enough that a few coats of paint will render it invisible. If the drawing disappears too soon the scene painter can always retrace over the sketch.

Black ink markers are useful for lettering, cartooning, and graphic effects that require thin black lines. Other colors can also be used, but it should be remembered that the thin lines produced by ink markers are too delicate to be read in larger auditoriums.

Tape, staples. Three-quarter-inch or one-inch-thick size masking tape is invaluable for a myriad of uses. A roll of tape is the sort of item that always disappears around a shop, so lots of rolls should be stocked. It is used to hold Kraft paper in place for masking, to hold brushes on extenders, tape acetate over elevations, mask out portions of stencils and so on. For heavy duty jobs (and for people who are not very good at taping a brush onto an extender anyway) a roll or two of duct tape or gaffer's tape should be kept around.

Since a drop cannot be laid down without staples, they should be stocked in quantity. Since almost any job using staples also involves removing them, the staples used should not be any longer than one-half inch or five-eighths inch. These should be more than sufficient for holding down most work without permanently entombing it in the shop.

Paper rolls. Brown Kraft paper comes in large rolls, and in different weights of paper. Light and medium weight Kraft paper are used for making pounces. Heavy weight paper is needed to lie under drops on the floor. (Bogus paper is also used for this purpose.) It is useful for covering counter tops, and sometimes is used for a drop cloth.

Polyethylene sheeting also comes in rolls in several weights. This thin plastic is often used for drop cloths, and for backing scrim when it is painted on the floor.

A small roll of acetate should be kept in the shop for protecting elevations or sketches. Tracing paper should also be stocked for designing stencil patterns.

Stencil paper. Stencil paper is an oily cardboard similar to that from which manila filing folders are made. The wax-like surface repels water, and it is light weight, which makes it useful for constructing stencils. It is an inexpensive material which is available in sheets. Some local paint stores stock it, or it can be obtained from theatrical suppliers.

Miscellaneous. Various other odd expendable bits are useful around the shop. A little hand cream is helpful for training brushes to stay in shape. Bar soap can be used to clean brushes (and painters). Paint thinner is infrequently needed, but invaluable for the odd, unexpected oil paint clean-up job. Elastic bands and twine are also useful for odd jobs such as binding brushes or rollers, or drawing a circle.

Tools You Can Buy   Although the paint brush is, perhaps, the most important scene painting tool, several others are necessary as well. Paint shops accumulate a lot of tools as they are needed for some show or other. Most of these tools were developed outside the theatre for some industrial or commercial use. Many theatrical materials have been developed this way. A theatre practitioner will notice some gadget that could solve a particular problem in the shop, and soon it has become a standard theatre shop item. An advantage that comes of this is that almost all of these tools can be found in local paint, garden, hardware, or other stores. Everyone discovers a favorite brand or type of gadget. The only criteria for choosing should be durability of the tool, and the availability of replacement parts, especially for tools like sprayers that have some parts that wear out frequently and see alot of use.

Free! About the only tools that you can get for free any more are paint can lid openers and mixing sticks. Most paint stores will include a few of each of these with a reasonably sized paint order. It is a good idea to collect can lid openers, and even chain one to the counter in the mixing area. It is the sort of small tool that is easily mislaid and vital when you are in a hurry. It saves a lot of wear and tear on the shop's screwdrivers as well. Even the most generous store proprietor will not be able to provide enough mixing sticks to service the shop adequately, but these commercial versions can serve as a model for a home-made version (constructed in great volume by a bored carpenter on a slow day). They are long, flat, and wide, like a paddle, so they will move as much paint in the can or bucket as possible. Round or squarish sticks are poor for mixing.

FIGURE 2–12. Paint mixer

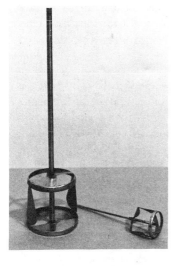

Mixer. There are several versions of the electric drill mixer on the market. This is a metal device attached to a long shaft, which is inserted into the chuck of an electric drill, and used in much the same way a handheld kitchen mixer is used. When purchasing one of these gadgets find one that presents the most possible mixing surface to the paint. A small, flat propeller will do very little good. The large sized mixers are great for mixing colors and reviving paint in five gallon buckets. A smaller one should be kept for five-quart buckets and for reviving gallon cans that have been left on the shelf too long.

Yardstick. Wooden yardsticks are commonly used as straight edges as well as for measuring. These used to be free items at paint and hardware stores, the name of the store imprinted on the wood so the painter would remember where to go back to buy more paint. Now you have to pay for the reminder, but not very much. The paint shop should have at least a half dozen of these in decent shape at any given time. They are among the most used tools, and the measuring markings disappear quickly under several layers of paint. When buying them the following hints should be kept in mind:

FIGURE 2–13. Yardsticks

1. Buy wood, not metal. Wood is rigid and light enough to be comfortably held in one hand.

2. Avoid nicks along the edges that will catch the brush and cause bumps in straight lines.

3. Sight along both edges of the stick to make sure it is not curved or warped. This will prevent inexplicably curved "straight" lines.

Containers. Many shops use any number of different containers for holding paint, but two choices are clearly superior: disposable metal cans and plastic containers.

Shops with access to a cafeteria kitchen can usually strike up a deal with the chef to save all the #10 and larger tin cans. The advantage to this, if the cans are plentiful, is that they are free, and after a show is painted they can be tossed out.

If cans are not available, the shop should stock plastic buckets and containers. Although metal buckets can last longer, plastic ones are much easier to clean. Five-quart buckets should be plentifully stocked for most jobs, as well as a smaller collection of five-gallon buckets for size or base color. In addition to buckets the shop should have several smaller containers with lids, to store detail colors and metallics. If people around the shop eat a lot of margarine they should be convinced to save the tubs. Freezer containers are also great for this purpose. They can be inexpensively obtained in hardware and grocery stores.

FIGURE 2–14. Snap line

Snap line. A snap line is a metal case with a reel of string in it, which also contains powdered chalk. The string is pulled out, stretched between two points, and snapped to produce a straight line of chalk. The string is then reeled back into the case for storage, or to pick up more chalk dust. The paint shop should have two or three of these gadgets. One should be filled with chalk (usually blue powdered chalk), for snapping lines on the floor or other areas where the line must stay for a while. The others should be filled with powdered charcoal for snapping guide lines on scenery that will eventually be removed.

Sponges. Aside from clean up, sponges are used for painting texture techniques. Therefore, the best kind of sponge to use is a natural sponge, with its rich, uneven texture. They are a trifle more expensive than synthetic sponges, but well worth the investment for the results obtained. Synthetic sponges are used for finer, more even textures. The hard edges should be tapered to avoid framed rectangle shapes being stamped on the scenery. Synthetic sponges can also be cut into patterns, or have shapes or textures cut into them.

FIGURE 2–15. Sponges: natural and synthetic

Pounce equipment. Aside from Kraft paper, a *pounce wheel* and a *pounce bag* are needed for pouncing. The pounce wheel is a small spiked wheel attached to a handle on an axle. It is available through theatrical supply companies, and is used to perforate lines into Kraft paper. Pounce bags are not commercially available, but they are very simple to make. They are sacks of porous cloth, often cheese cloth, filled with powdered charcoal. The bag is drawn closed with an elastic band. Light weight muslin makes excellent pounce bags.

FIGURE 2–16. Pounce wheel and pounce bag

Sprayers. Various sprayers are useful for a number of purposes in scene painting. The simplest is the *mister* bottle, manufactured for moistening house plants. These are used with water to feather out, or soften, paint lines (as in marble veining), or can be used with thin paint for fine spattering over small areas.

Pump sprayers are probably the most useful type of sprayer for scene painting. They are manufactured for spraying insecticide on shrubbery and outdoor plants. They are light, self-contained, and portable. They come in two- or four-gallon sizes, and are manufactured by a number of companies, the best-known brand being the Hudson sprayer.

The sprayer consists of three main parts: the tank, the hose and nozzle, and the pump. The tank is filled with thinned paint, dye, size, and so on, leaving enough room for some air on top. Whatever is put in should be strained first, because the nozzle easily clogs. A perfect strainer for this purpose is a kitchen flour sifter. The pump is then attached, and the air in the tank is pressurized by pumping the handle up and down. Ample air pressure is achieved when it becomes difficult to push the plunger back into the pump. Paint is then sprayed out the nozzle in a stream or mist by pressing a trigger.

In addition to straining the paint it is important to clean the sprayer carefully after each use. The hose and nozzle will clog if given the opportunity, and the paint hardens the rubber or cork seals. Some models of pump sprayer are made out of stainless steel and, although they cost more, they will last forever if reasonably cared for, so are worth the expense. Repair kits containing spare seals, springs, and nozzle ends are sold, and a few should be kept in the shop for each sprayer. When a pump will not build up sufficient pressure it probably needs new gaskets. The cylinder should be removed—some brands unscrew, some must be pryed off—and the leather or rubber gasket removed from the piston, usually accomplished by turning a hex nut. The small gasket on the bottom of the cylinder should also be replaced. If there is a washer at the top of the cylinder where the pump closes onto the top of the tank, it should be replaced as well. To repair a leaky nozzle all the washers in it should be replaced. If the hose develops a leak, it can be removed by loosening its clamps and replaced with a new one.

FIGURE 2–17. Pump sprayer, pneumatic sprayer, plant mister

A third type of sprayer is the *pneumatic sprayer*. Like the pump sprayer this device uses pressurized air to push the paint through a nozzle, but because its compressor can create a good deal more air pressure, and a steadier supply of it than can a pump sprayer, it can produce a much finer mist of paint. This air-brush effect is often too fine to read as a texture in theatrical scene painting, although it is often used with wallpaper stencils to produce well defined patterns. The guidelines for caring for a pump sprayer apply to pneumatic sprayers with the addition that the pressure valve must be closely watched. If too much pressure builds up in the tank the scene painter could literally experience an explosion of color.

Rollers.   Paint rollers, inexpensively sold in paint and hardware stores, can be used for several texture techniques. The smaller size (2-inch) is useful, as well as the regular sized ones. One way to get an unusual texture from a roller is to wrap twine around it. Binding it in different patterns will produce unlimited possibilities for textures. Roller handles and trays are permanent equipment. Spare rollers (tubes) should be kept in stock. Although these can be cleaned, they wear out fairly quickly and need to be replaced frequently.

FIGURE 2–18. Trammel heads

Trammel heads.   Trammel heads are small brackets that clamp onto a length of wood and hold a metal point or a pencil. They are used for drawing circles the same way a beam compass is used. The metal point head is clamped the desired distance (the radius of the circle) from the pencil head. The point is placed at the center point, and the pencil head arced around it. With care a charcoal stick can be used in place of a pencil, but it will break very easily. A solution to this problem is to use a charcoal pencil instead.

FIGURE 2–19. Feather duster

Palette trays.   For small mixing jobs and other assorted uses plastic cafeteria trays make the best *palettes*. They are used most often for detail painting when smaller amounts of paints are mixed in several shades. They should be cleaned well after each use so old paint does not mix with new.

Feather dusters.   Feather dusters, available at most hardware stores, are used to apply a random but even texture over a large area. The feather duster is dipped into a palette tray filled with paint, then stippled onto the scenery. Each feather leaves a separate impression, which creates a textured look. Care should be taken not to break the feathers, but otherwise the duster can be washed and cared for just like a brush.

FIGURE 2-20.
Whisk broom, scrub brush

FIGURE 2-21. A basic set
of foam carving knives

Whisk brooms. A whisk broom, when dragged through wet scenic dope, creates three-dimensional wood-grain effects. Stippling with a whisk broom produces a completely different texture. (They are also handy for cleaning off counter tops.) It should be cleaned in luke warm water before the dope has had an opportunity to dry. Scrub brushes, wire brushes, and other stiff-bristled brushes can also be used to create all sorts of interesting textures in dope.

Knives, hot wires. A large kitchen knife, a small paring knife, and an oyster knife make a good basic set of foam carving tools. The former two knives are used for cutting sharp edges, and making distinct gouges. The oyster knife is used to gouge out rough foam chips. Table model or hand held *hot wires* are also used for cutting foam. These should only be used in a well-ventilated space, because when foam is heated it creates toxic fumes. Hot wires are available commercially, and are also fairly easy to build in the shop.

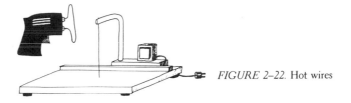

FIGURE 2-22. Hot wires

FIGURE 2-23. Foam rubber
paint applicators

Foam rubber applicators. Foam rubber paint applicators are used for applying paint, and make great glue brush substitutes. They are especially useful for applying an even coat of contact cement that holds foam to wood scenery. This cement (and eventually any glue) ruins brushes pretty quickly, but the foam applicators are so cheap they can be tossed away without a twinge of budgetary guilt whenever one hardens. For painting they may be used as is, or cut to produce patterns or hatch lines.

Tools You Can Build and How to Build Them

A number of scene painting tools can be inexpensively built in the shop. Some of these are for specialized jobs, but many are used as frequently as any you can buy. Most of these tools can be built with easy-to-find materials that can be bought in any locality.

Straightedge. It is important to have good *straightedges* in the shop. These are used with liners for lining. First of all, a straightedge should be straight. It is essential that the wood be sighted along the edge or edges that will be used to make sure it is not warped. The usable edge or edges are bevelled along their length. When painting with a straightedge the brush is held perpendicularly to the straightedge and guided along the edge. The bevelled bottom prevents the bottom of the bristles from actually touching the wood, which prevents the paint from seeping under the wood, causing dripping and splotching.

To build:

1. Cut a four-to-six-foot-long length of 1 by 3. (Carefully check to make sure it is not warped.)

2. On a table saw, bevel the edges. Do not bevel the edges to a sharp point, but leave about a quarter of an inch of straight side near the top. When bevelling both sides the bevel should be wider at the top and narrower on the bottom of both sides, so the bevels appear to be mirror images of each other.

3. Fasten a handle securely to the top where the straight edge will balance evenly.

For painting up:

Screw a screen door handle into the top of the straight edge.

For painting down:

Cut a handle out of 1 by 3, three or four feet tall, depending on what feels comfortable to the individual. Glue the handle on, and screw through the bottom of the straightedge. Triangular braces provide added strength.

FIGURE 2–24. Straightedges

FIGURE 2–25. Drawing stick

Drawing stick. Drawing sticks are used for charcoal drawing when painting down. They are made of thin bamboo, and act as long handles to hold the vine charcoal for drawing long continuous lines on scenery without having to kneel to do so.

To build:

1. Cut a thin wand of bamboo about four feet long (adjust length to individual height).

2. Cut the joint off one end so a long (about four to six inches) hollow length is opened on one end.

3. Carefully cut with a knife or band saw triangular notches about two inches long into the open end, creating three or four "teeth."

4. Insert a stick of charcoal into the notched end.

5. Wrap the "teeth" with an elastic band so they bite into the charcoal, holding it in place.

Brush extender. When painting on the floor, long light-weight handles are attached to the brush handles so the scene painter can avoid stooping to paint, and can paint long, sweeping lines. Commercial aluminum extenders are sold, and broom sticks can be used, although they tend to be a bit heavy. A simple bamboo brush extender can be built easily. Because bamboo is so lightweight it is easy to use.

To build:

1. Cut a three- or four-foot length of bamboo at the joints so that both ends are closed (for strength, and to avoid splintering).

2. Wrap one end with duct tape. (If that end should splinter the tape protects the scene painter's hands. Splintered bamboo is as sharp as a knife. This tape also prevents the bamboo from splintering further.)

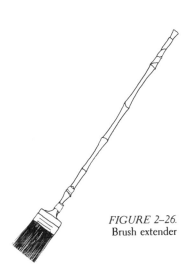

FIGURE 2-26.
Brush extender

3. Firmly tape the brush handle to the other end of the extender with masking tape or duct tape. The brush and the extender must be dry when this is done, so the tape will stick.

Snap line. There are several variations on the basic idea of the snap line. The simplest is to rub a length of string with a thick stick of charcoal, stretch the string between two points as tightly as possible, and snap it to produce a charcoal line. Many scene painters prefer the bow variety, especially for painting up. This gadget looks somewhat like an archery bow, and works in the same way. The string is rubbed with a large stick of charcoal, then the bow is lined up with two points on the scenery. It is held with one hand and snapped with the other. The bow snap line is the only variety that is easily used by one person.

To build:

1. Cut a straight 1 by 2 of clear pine to about six feet, or any desired length. Six feet is managable.

2. Cut two isosceles triangles out of 1-by hardwood stock. Soft wood will cause problems. The equal sides should be two or three inches long.

3. On the end of one side of each triangle (not the 90 degree angle!) cut a very short notch (1/32-inch should be enough).

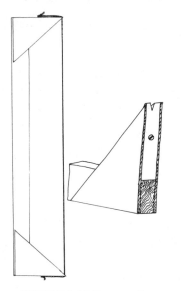

FIGURE 2–27. Bow snap line

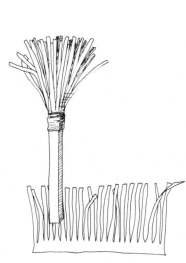

FIGURE 2–28. Flog

4. Fasten one triangle (notch up) to each end of the 1 by 2 so the edge of the 90 degree angle becomes a continuation of the edge of the board. Use white glue and screws (remember hardwood must be predrilled to avoid splitting). When facing up, the finished construction should look like an extremely elongated "u."

5. Screw a small wood screw into each end of the 1 by 2. Do not screw it in all the way, let about one-quarter inch stick out.

6. Firmly knot one end of the string onto one of the screws. String it through the notches, stretch tightly, then fasten it to the screw on the other side. Retighten or replace the string as needed.

Flog. A flog is used to erase charcoal from scenery. It consists of fabric strips fastened to a wooden handle. The charcoal is beaten, or flogged, off the scenery with the fabric strips (take care not to hit the scenery with the handle, because it may tear).

To build:

1. Cut out a 12-inch by 18-inch rectangle of muslin or canvas.

2. Along one of the 18-inch edges cut starter cuts about every half inch with a pair of scissors.

3. Rip strips of fabric from the starter cuts, leaving about a two-inch band along the bottom edge, which keeps the individual strips attached to each other.

4. Cut a dowel or 1 by 1 about one foot long (three or four feet long for working down).

5. Staple one end of the bottom band of fabric to an end of the handle.

6. Wrap the rest of the band around the end of the handle. When completely wrapped, staple again so it cannot unravel.

7. Wrap the band with duct tape to protect the scene painters' hands from the staples.

Stencils. Stencils are patterns cut out of stiff paper through which paint is applied. They are most often used for creating the effect of wallpaper on scenery. The size and shape is determined by the design of the pattern. A detailed discussion of their construction and use is in chapter seven.

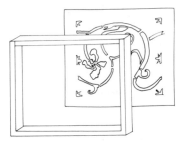

FIGURE 2–29. Stencil

To build:

1. Cut design out of stencil paper (available at paint stores or scene paint suppliers). Leave at least a three-inch border between the end of the design and the edge of the paper.

2. Make a rectangular frame out of 1 by 1 pine. The outside edge of the pine should exactly match the size of the stencil paper.

3. Paint a layer of white glue along one side of the frame, and fasten the stencil paper over the wet glue with a staple gun.

4. Shellac both sides of the stencil paper, one at a time, letting the first side dry before shellacking the other.

5. For stencils with large cut-out areas, like long wallpaper stripes, fasten picture-hanging wire from one side of the frame to the other on both sides to help support the stencil paper.

Foam rubber stamps. Foam rubber stamps can be cut to any pattern and used to stamp repeats quickly to paint gardens, trees, forests, stones, or any number of items. Like stencils, they are custom made for a particular use in a show. They should be saved, however, because they can be used again and again if they are well constructed. Old stamps can be used in different colors and combinations and are not usually as easily recognizable from show to show as stencils are.

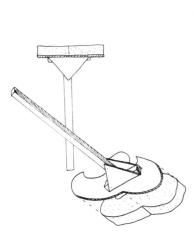

FIGURE 2–30. Foam rubber stamp

To build:

1. Cut silhouette of stamp design out of one-inch-thick foam rubber. Cut or tear the inside of the design to create textures or details within the silhouette (such as the veins of a leaf).

2. Lay foam shape on a piece of one-quarter-inch or three-eights-inch plywood. Trace the silhouette onto the wood.

3. Cut out the plywood shape on a band saw.

4. Attach the plywood shape to a handle. (See instructions for attaching handles to straight edges.)

5. Using a good contact cement, line up and fasten the foam shape to the plywood replica. Test the contact cement on a scrap of foam rubber first, because some cements melt it.

Compass. Two homemade compasses can work well for drawing large circles. One simply consists of a length of string.

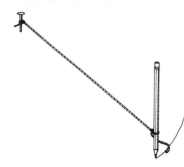

FIGURE 2-31. String compass

FIGURE 2-32. Board compass

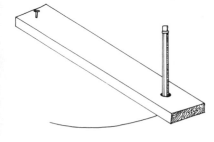

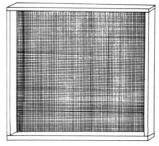

FIGURE 2-33. Transfer screen

One end is tied to a nail. The string is measured the length of the radius, where a loop is tied. The nail is tacked part way in at the center point. A stick of charcoal is placed in the loop, and, keeping the string tight while moving the charcoal around the center point, the circle is drawn. Care must be taken to use string that does not stretch.

The second method works on the same principle, but is a little more accurate because it uses a rigid board. A hole is drilled in one end of a board. The length of the radius is measured down the board, and a nail is driven through that point. The nail is then lightly tacked into the center point, and the circle is drawn with a stick of charcoal stuck through the hole. This compass can be reused for different sized circles by moving the nail.

Transfer screen. A transfer screen is a framed square of scrim. It is used for tracing drawings or patterns at one location on scenery, and redrawing them exactly at another. The screen is placed on the scenery over the original drawing. This drawing can be seen through the scrim gauze, and is traced onto it with charcoal. The screen is then placed on the scenery where the pattern is to be repeated, and the drawing is gone over again with charcoal. The charcoal goes through the scrim onto the surface of the scenery. To reverse a pattern the same method is used, but before redrawing the screen is turned over.

To build:

1. Construct a three or four foot square frame out of 1 by 2. Use lap joints at the corners, or indent corner blocks for strength.

2. Glue and staple sharkstooth scrim to the frame. Make sure it is stretched on tightly.

3 Color and paint

Although scene paint comes in a variety of colors, it is almost always necessary to mix them to get just the right one. The painting of scenery involves more than just choosing a color out of the can and painting it on. Several colors are chosen that form a palette that will blend into a sensible, visually pleasing color scheme. The viewer's perception of each color is affected by all the other colors in the palette, and they must relate to one another in a way that makes visual sense.

Often the scenic designer will provide color swatches on the painter's elevations. This does not mean the colors should be slavishly copied and just painted in the right spots. The scenic artist must exercise some judgment when mixing the colors, and must have at least some basic knowledge of color theory. As a palette is being developed there are several questions about it that should be answered. Examples: Do the colors relate well to one another? Will bright stage lighting substantially change the look of the colors? Will warm-colored lights turn cool-colored paint black? Will a highlight color look natural compared to the blend and shade colors?

First, it is helpful to define "color." We refer to a rose as red, but how do we distinguish its red from that of a fire engine or a sunset? When we refer to a color we are alluding to its hue, its value, and its purity.

Hue refers to what we commonly call colors, such as red, blue, green, and so on. In the case of the rose, it is the quality of the flower that causes us to label it red.

The *value* of that red is its black-to-white relationship. A pink rose, for example, has a fairly light value, while its hue is still called "red."

43

FIGURE 3–1.
Color wheel

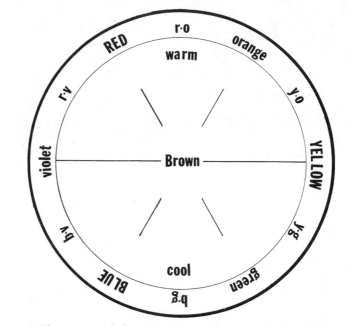

The *purity* of the red refers to how much of other colors are in it. A magenta rose, aside from being a horticultural anomaly, may still be referred to as red in hue, but its purity is not very high because of the blue in it. The predominant color determines the hue. Thus, a purple rose that tends toward red is red in hue, even though there is almost the same amount of blue in it, and vice versa. So the hue of the rose tells us what color it is, and its value and purity tell us what kind of that color it is.

The *color wheel* is a chart that helps to sort out one color from another. It is a logical arrangement of all the colors, according to their characteristics. Because it illustrates relationships of colors to each other it is invaluable as an aid to creating a good palette.

The *primary colors* in pigment are red, blue, and yellow. They are called primary colors because they cannot be made by mixing other colors together. You either have them or you do not. The primaries are equally spaced along the circumference of the wheel, dividing it into thirds.

A *secondary color* is the color that results from mixing equal portions of any two primary colors. By mixing red and yellow you get the secondary color orange. You get green by mixing yellow and blue, and violet by mixing blue and red. Each secondary color is placed halfway between the two primaries it is comprised of, dividing the color wheel into equal sixths. The tertiaries (yellow-green, yellow-orange, red-orange, and so on) are placed halfway between the primary and secondary that, when mixed in equal parts, comprise them. Infinitely more colors can be added this way, but for normal use it is not necessary to go beyond the tertiaries.

Now a line can be drawn across the diameter of the circle that crosses yellow and violet, the color directly opposite it. All the colors on the side of the line where red is are referred to as *warm colors*. The colors on the blue side of the line are called *cool colors*. The colors that are right on the line are called *neutral colors*. A neutral color seems warm when placed next to a cool color, and cool when placed next to a warm.

So far we have worked with mixing hue along the circumference of the wheel. It is also possible to mix through it, which changes the purity of the hues. If the three primaries are mixed in equal portions the result will be a neutral brown. The warm red and cool blue neutralize each other, and yellow is a neutral color. The same brown should result when the three secondaries are equally mixed, or, indeed, any three colors that are equally spaced along the circumference of the wheel (assuming the colors are pure). Many different kinds of brown will result by mixing the colors from the circumference unequally. It is, therefore, possible to have warm browns and cool browns. Some examples are burnt umber (a relatively neutral brown), raw umber (a greenish or cool brown), and burnt sienna (a reddish or warm brown).

Every color on the circumference of the color wheel lies directly across (a diameter) from another color. Such colors are called *opposite colors*. Examples of opposite colors are red and green, yellow and violet, and blue-violet and yellow-orange. When opposite colors are mixed equally they will form a kind of dull gray. This is useful to know, because when a color in the scene painting palette is too bright it can be dulled a bit by adding a little of its opposite color. The more of the opposite color is added, the duller it will become, until it begins to look muddy toward the center of the wheel. Scene painters do not go running to look at a color wheel every five minutes, but there is a trick for finding opposite colors without using one. For example, when trying to find the opposite of yellow, stare at a patch of yellow for about a minute, then quickly look away, at something white. By an optical illusion a violet patch appears (the same size and shape as the actual yellow patch). This trick works for all colors.

Black, white, and grays interact with the hues represented on the color wheel to change their value. Maroon is a red with some dark gray in it, and pink is red mixed with white. As hues can be changed by black and/or white, so can hues change grays. Neutral gray is made from equal portions of black and white, or from black and white in any proportion and a neutral color. (Black and white are also neutral, neither being warm or cool by itself.) Warm grays are made by mixing black and white and a warm color, and cool grays by substituting a cool for the warm.

Since warm and cool colors are often used in perspective painting to suggest three-dimensional objects or spaces, it is important to be able to distinguish between them. A flat scene painted with warm and cool grays can create a very convincing illusion of distance. The balance of warm to cool colors can be used very effectively, even in monochromatic scenes (scenes that are painted in all warm or all cool colors). For example, red-violet and red-orange are both very warm colors, but red-violet is closer to the cool range on the color wheel, because it has a little blue in it. This means it is cooler than the red-orange, and the two colors relate in a monochromatic scene in much the same way that obviously warm and cool colors like red and blue relate in a polychromatic one.

MIXING PAINT

All of this color theory has real value when creating the palette for a set. A show's palette is the combination of colors chosen for it. The palette should be kept limited so the eye is not assaulted by too many unrelated colors, and should be carefully chosen to make the appropriate visual statement. When mixing paint the scene painter should also have some knowledge of the properties of paint, how pigment reacts with light, and the compatibility of different paints and other substances.

Before painting on the actual set all the colors to be used on it should be tested on materials similar to those that the scenery is made of. Left over scraps from the set are the best, because the paint will do exactly on the test what it will do on the scenery. Large color swatches should be painted on the test in the same relationships they will be used in on stage. There are a number of reasons why this is important.

First, most paints dry a shade or two lighter than they appear when they are wet (their value changes). If white is mixed into a color, the color will dry several shades lighter. Thus it is poor practice to rely on the colors in their buckets when putting together a palette, because the wet paint is not the same color it will be when it is dry.

Second, a person's perception of an individual color is changed by the colors around it. Colors appear brighter against a dark background than they do against a light one. The same color, when surrounded by different colors in different parts of the set, may appear to be two different colors. The relationships of all the colors within the palette for a show can be a very delicate balance which can be thrown off by one wrong color.

Finally, the test swatches should be tested under the anticipated colors of light. Light color and pigment color mix subtractively to produce a third color that is perceived by the audience. For example a stage light with a red filter on it allows only the red wavelengths to pass through, eliminating all the other colors in white light. (White light is made up of all the colors in the spectrum. The light color wheel differs from the pigment wheel in that all the colors on its circumference make white, not brown, when mixed together.) When this red light hits an object that is painted violet, the red in the color is reflected, but the blue does not react. The resultant color is a dark red. If the same red light hits a blue object it will appear black (an absence of color), because there is no blue in the light rays to react with the pigment. This suggests that even when a monochromatic look is desired some warms and cools should be worked into the color scheme, while keeping the impression of a monochromatic scene by favoring either warms or cools.

When mixing colors it is important to remember color theory, and to apply it directly. To brighten a color it should be highly saturated (very pure) with its basic hue, and neutral in value. Opposite colors are used to dull each other. Care should be taken when mixing warm or cool grays or browns not to dull them into oblivion. When mixing light and shadow colors it is useful to begin with the neutral color. In this context the term neutral means the "real" color of the object. Assuming a warm light source such as the sun, the shadow color might be a blue-gray mixed with the neutral, and the highlight a yellowish-white, also mixed with the neutral. Because the three colors have the neutral in common they visually relate well. Any old cool color for shadow or warm for light will not necessarily make sense when related to a specific neutral color.

Sometimes so much of a color is needed that it does not fit into one bucket. Even when great care is taken to add equal parts of each color to two or more buckets the result will probably be different shades of the same color in each bucket. To prevent this from happening the buckets are *boxed* after the color has been mixed into each of them. If two buckets that are to have the same paint have been filled, half of each is poured into a third bucket. The remaining half of the first is poured into the second. The two resultant buckets are stirred, then the process is repeated two or three times. Boxing the paint will insure that a color is the same throughout the whole set.

No scene painter is ever happy about running out of a color too soon. It is pretty frustrating to run out of the base color for a set, but it is a common problem that is not impossible to solve. The key to matching a new batch of color to the old one is in doing it while there is still some wet paint left. Since paint dries a few shades lighter it is a lot easier to match it wet. Therefore, the new paint should be mixed while some of the old paint is still wet. The new batch should be mixed in a separate bucket. When it appears to be the same color as the old one, a mixing stick should be dipped into the new, and another into the old. A few drops of paint should be allowed to drip from one stick to the other. If the drops disappear, the colors match perfectly. This usually does not happen on the first try. It is apparent that one color is warmer, cooler, or brighter. That, and a knowledge of color theory, suggests what color or colors need to be added to match the original batch of color.

Most shops end up with a number of different kinds of paint, and the temptation is to mix them together, especially when a particular color is used up in the type of paint generally being used. Here it is necessary to note that not all paints are compatible. As a general rule water-based paints should never be mixed with oil-based ones. They repel each other, making an even spread impossible to achieve. Most scene paint is water based, but some binders used in them are not compatible. As always, the best practice is to test a small amount on the side to see what it does. For example, some binders used to make pigment paint will not mix well with latex, causing the color to streak unevenly. (This can be a very nice effect when planned for, but can also be a nasty surprise.) In general, the best practice is not to mix different paints at all. The reason that several types of paint are used in the theatre is that each one has specific characteristics that make it desirable for a special purpose. Their effectiveness is undermined or eliminated when they are indiscriminately blended.

Mixing aniline dye colors is different from paint color mixing. The purpose of using dyes is that they are very clear and brilliant. Many of the colors become grayed and muddy when mixed together. It is best not to mix them, but simply to use the commercially available colors as is, like crayons are used in a coloring book (by a neat child). Experimentation will show that some of the colors do mix well. Letting one color dry, then painting over it with another also works for some of the colors, preserving the brilliance of the dye.

Some scene paint is prepackaged, and other kinds have to be mixed from scratch. Knowledge of what paint is and how it works allows the scene painter to get the most out of it. Some paints work well on certain materials but not on others, or for a certain purpose. For example, paint used on the floor of a set must hold on better than paint used on walls. In a show that involves throwing water or food around, or in which a lot of stage blood is "shed" the paint must be insoluble after it has dried, and easy to clean off as well.

Paint is made up of three elements: *pigment, binder,* and *medium.*

Pigment is simply colored powder. The purpose of painting is to somehow get the pigment onto the scenery in the desired spot, and make it stay there. Pigment comes in two basic categories: earth colors and dye colors. Earth colors are literally what their name implies—colored earth. Many of these are named for their places of origin such as Sienna or Umber. Scene painting colors that are included in this category are yellow ochre, raw and burnt umber, raw and burnt sienna, van dyke brown, brown lake, venetian red, indian red, and zinc white. Dye colors are produced either synthetically, or from mineral pigment. Because of the processing and substances needed to produce them they are more expensive to buy than earth colors. The more brilliant colors are included among the dye colors also. They include yellow, orange, vermillian, turkey red lake, bright red, magenta, purple, violet, ultramarine blue, cobalt blue, prussian blue, cerulean blue, turquoise, chrome oxide green, and emerald green.

Binder is a substance that adheres the pigment to the surface that is being painted. Various glues, rubbers, and vinyls are used for binder.

The medium in paint is the liquid in which the other two elements are mixed and permits them to flow easily onto the surface of the scenery. When paint dries the medium evaporates, leaving only the binder and pigment. Water and oil are the most common mediums used in paint.

The characteristics of a particular paint are determined by the combination of its pigment, medium, and, especially, the binder. Some binders are stronger than others, some dry shinier, and some are insoluble after they dry. When choosing which type of paint to use the look and usage of each piece of scenery must be considered. Water-repellent paints should be used to paint scenery for outdoor theatres. A strong binder should be used on all floors and stairways, especially in shows that involve a lot of dancing. Binders that dry with a dull finish should be used on most scenery, but sometimes a glossy finish is wanted for woodwork, tile, or furniture.

BINDERS, SIZES, DOPES

Making binders, sizes, and dopes is the first step in making paint. These substances have other uses as well. Binders are adhesives as we have discussed. Size is a mixture of binder and medium. When pigment is added to size the result is paint. Size is also used to stretch and seal scenic fabrics, providing an even, nonabsorbent surface to paint on. Size that has been mixed in the correct proportions for making paint is called working size. A supply of this size is kept in the shop when a lot of paint is being made. Scenic dope is size with some thickening agent in it. It is used to create textured surfaces of different kinds, and, as with size, pigment can be added to it to create very thick paint.

There are two categories of binders these days: the old and the new style. The old style binders have to be mixed in the shop, usually on the stove. The advantage to using them is that the scene painter has total control over the composition of the paint. The new ones are premixed binders, and can be watered down or thickened at room temperature, without any special preparations. They are more convenient to use. Here is how the categories roughly relate to each other:

OLD	NEW	CHARACTERISTICS
Gelatine Glue	White Glue, Casein	Good, consistent drying binder
Carpenter's Glue	Vinyl	Stronger binder
Flexible Glue	Latex, Vinyl	Dries flexible, which is necessary for soft scenery that often may be bunched up or folded
Dextrine	Clear Vinyl	Good for mixing metallics

Paint shops seem to be moving toward using predominantly newer forms of binders for convenience, but because the old types are so inexpensive they are still used extensively. When choosing a binder for the paint shop consider the man-hours needed to make the glue as part of its cost, not to mention the fuss, smell, and extra equipment. Using the old kind of binders actually may turn out to be more expensive than using the premixed kinds in shops where the scene painters are paid by the hour. They tend to be more cost effective in community or educational theatres.

When making size it must be tested to make sure there is enough binder in it, but not too much. This is done by sticking the thumb and forefinger into the size, and pressing them together as it dries. If the size is properly proportioned the skin of the two fingers will stick a bit as they are gently pulled apart, then separate. If the fingers do not stick at all more glue is needed—if they will not come apart more water is indicated. (It is unlikely that they will be so stuck that they are actually glued together. If this happens they can be separated by running warm or hot water over them. While waiting for his or her fingers to come apart, the scene painter can contemplate how badly the size recipe has been bungled.)

Gelatine Glue

Gelatine glue is made from animal hooves, and is essentially the same stuff that old-fashioned stage lighting gels and Jell-o are made of. It is inexpensive, uniform, and mixes well with other water-based binders. It comes in powder, grains, or crystals, is buff colored, and is gritty to the touch. It must be cooked on the stove, and before too long it begins to smell terrible, so only what is needed immediately should be mixed at a time. Usually the lowest person on the totem pole gets to oversee the glue pot.

Glue Recipe:
1. Place the amount of glue that is wanted into a double boiler.
2. Pour in water until glue is covered. Allow to soak overnight.
3. Heat in a double boiler until glue is dissolved.

Working Size:
1. Add one part glue to ten parts water.
2. Stir and test.

Carpenter's Glue

Carpenter's glue is sometimes referred to as "ground glue," which can be confusing because gelatine glue is sometimes called "ground flake glue." It is inexpensive, and comes in granulated or crystal form. It is stronger than gelatine glue, so it can safely be diluted more, but it is a less consistent and less flexible binder. It looks a lot like gelatine glue, so if both are stocked they should be well labeled.

Glue Recipe:

1. Place the amount of glue that is wanted into a double boiler.
2. Pour in water until glue is covered. Allow to soak overnight.
3. Heat until glue is dissolved.

Working Size:

1. Add one part premixed glue to sixteen parts water.
2. Stir and test.

Flexible Glue This binder is called what it is: flexible. It is excellent for painting soft scenery that must be rolled or folded, because paint made from it will not crack. A rubber-based glue, it is compatible with latex, and makes a good deck paint when whiting is added for thickening. It is sold in cakes and slabs.

Glue Recipe:

1. Cover a slab of glue with water and soak for an hour.
2. Heat in a double boiler until the glue has melted.

Working Size:

1. Add one part premixed glue to ten parts water.
2. Stir and test.

There is a version of this glue called polyvinyl flexible cold-water glue that can be mixed directly into the working size without cooking it:

Working Size:

1. Add one part glue powder to five parts water.
2. Stir and test.

White Glue White glue is a popular carpentry glue available at any local hardware store. It comes in tiny 1-1/4-ounce bottles, fifty-gallon drums, and many sizes in between. It is a premixed glue, so the scene painter is spared the stove and the smell. At full strength it dries hard and clear, and glossy. When preparing size enough water must be added so that it will not dry to a glossy finish. Some brands of white glue dry flexible, instead of rigid. It always seems that a lot of water is added to not very much glue when making size, but testing will show that the binder is sufficient. It is more expensive than gelatine glue, but the savings in time and mess are worth it to many scene painters. White glue is a thick, sticky white liquid when wet. It is not a bad idea to keep some at full strength in plastic squeeze bottles for small gluing jobs, such as gluing a handle onto a stamp.

There is a stronger version of white glue on the market called carpenter's glue. It is packaged the same as white glue, and has the same characteristics, except that it is stronger and buff colored instead of white.

Working Size:

1. Mix one part white glue to ten parts water.
2. Stir and test. (Stir well. The white glue is heavier than the water, and size made from it should be stirred frequently.)

Starch Corn starch or laundry starch, both inexpensively available in grocery stores, make very good size that uniformly stretches and seals muslin or canvas. Starch is the only size that should be used on muslin for stained-glass-window effects. It comes in a box in powdered form, and when it dries the fabric feels stiff and brittle like paper. When using starch with analine dyes some methocel should be added so the dyes will not bleed over the fabric. Starch is also compatible with glue and vinyl sizes.

Corn Starch Size:

1. Boil four gallons of water*
2. Dissolve a box of corn starch in one-half gallon of luke warm water from the sink.
3. Pour the dissolved starch into the boiling water and stir. The quality of the starch will turn milky fairly soon.
4. Remove from the heat and allow to cool. Cooling can be sped up by putting the bucket of hot starch into a tub of cold water. Do not let the water get into the starch.
5. Strain thoroughly before using.

*For thick starch for stained glass use half as much boiling water.

Laundry Starch Size:

1. Boil three gallons of water*
2. Dissolve a one pound box of starch (gloss starch only!) in one-half gallon of lukewarm water from the sink.

*For thick starch use only one gallon of boiling water.

3. Remove the boiling water from the stove, and stir in the dissolved starch.

4. Allow to cool.

5. Strain thoroughly before using.

Clear Liquid Latex and Vinyl

Latex is a rubber- or plastic-based binder, and vinyl a plastic base. Both are premixed liquids and come in one-gallon cans. They come in a choice of finishes: gloss, semigloss, and flat. Latex is not absorbed into fabric, but forms a rubbery waterproof layer on top of it. Vinyl has more or less replaced dextrine for mixing bronzing powders. Both are fairly flexible.

Working Size, Latex:

1. Add one part clear liquid latex to two parts water.*

2. Stir and test.

Working Size, Vinyl:

1. Add one part clear liquid vinyl to five parts water.

2. Stir and test.

*The amount of water that can be added varies according to what brand you buy. Add less water for thinner clear vinyl or latex.

Wheat Paste

Wheat paste is used to adhere wallpaper to hard covered flats. It is the same wheat paste that kindergarten children use. It comes in a box in powdered form.

Glue Recipe:

1. Mix two pounds of wheat paste powder into five quarts of warm or cool water.

2. Stir thoroughly until all the lumps are gone.

Scenic Dopes

Scenic dope is thick goo that is used for three dimensional texturing on scenery. Bricks, wood grain, rosettes, and leading for stained-glass windows are just a few examples of what it can be used for. It can be made from gelatine glue or white glue using whiting as a thickener, or it can be made with commercial powders. There are also premixed goos such as topping compound available in paint stores and lumber yards.

It can be applied with a brush, putty knife, squeeze bottle, or by hand, and textures are impressed into it with wire brushes, whisk brooms, stamps, or templates.

Recipe for Gelatine Glue Dope:

Gelatine glue dope must be applied to scenery warm or hot. When it cools it hardens, but it can be made pliable again by reheating it.

1. Add one part premixed gelatine glue to three parts hot water.
2. Stir in two parts whiting.
3. Keep warm while using.

For thicker dope use two parts hot water and three parts whiting. For thinner dope use four parts hot water and one part whiting. Adjust the thickness as appropriate.

Recipe for White Glue Dope:

This version of scenic dope need not be kept warm, which makes it easier to use, but once it dries, that is it. Batches in progress should be kept wet, and covered when not in use.

1. Add one part white glue to three parts water.
2. Stir in three parts whiting.

For thicker dope use more whiting, and use less for thinner dope.

One of many commercial dopes is topping compound. This is a surprisingly inexpensive latex-based goop that comes premixed in one- or five-gallon containers. Anyone who has been in an Italian restaurant with "stucco" walls has seen at least one topping compound technique.

In the bucket it comes pretty thick. It is grayish-white in its wet form, but dries white like plaster. It can be thinned with water, and tools can be cleaned in warm water. It dries somewhat brittle, and may crack if the surface it is applied to is not completely rigid.

There are two approaches to coloring scenic dope. The first is to simply paint over it after it has dried. This choice is appropriate when using an involved technique using several colors or brush strokes. The second is to mix color into the dope itself. Pigment or paint can be stirred right into the dope before it is applied to the set. Mixing gray paint into thick dope for window leading is one example of this technique.

Cements for Attaching Foams

Sometimes foam is adhered to scenery in the paint shop where it is worked or carved. There are two adhesives that are commonly used for this purpose.

Mastik is a tan-colored goo, available in gallon cans. It is used by house carpenters to hold paneling onto walls. For scenic use it can be aggravating stuff, for if it's not used just right the foam falls off, usually in the middle of carving it. Part of the reason for this is that it is put on in patches. When foam is carved through its entire thickness, care must be taken not to carve a part that is not directly held on. Often, too, the pressure exerted while carving is too great for the bond. The advantage is that it is readily available in local hardware stores.

To use:

1. Make sure both surfaces to be joined are clean and dry.
2. With a putty knife, scoop on the mastic, about every six inches.
3. Press the foam tightly into place.

The 3-M company makes a contact cement called "Fast Bond-30" which is a superior product for adhering foam to wood or other foam. It produces a very strong bond without eating away the foam. It comes in white or green liquid in one- or five-gallon cans. The green version is preferable because many foams are white, so it is hard to see where the cement has already been applied and where more needs to be put on. When used correctly it makes a most satisfactory permanent bond.

To use:

1. Make sure both surfaces to be joined are clean and dry.
2. Brush contact cement onto both surfaces. (A foam rubber paint applicator is great for this job.)
3. Wait for the cement to dry on both surfaces. This takes about twenty minutes, after which time the color of the contact cement becomes slightly darker.
4. Carefully line up the two surfaces and press firmly together. Make sure they are lined up perfectly before allowing them to touch each other—this is strong cement! (The surfaces will not stick at all if the cement is still wet. Because the foam is not very porous, air cannot get in to dry it. Also if the cement has been left out to dry too long, it won't stick. Twenty minutes is about right. (Less time if you use a fan.) The cement dries faster on wood than it does on foam because wood is more porous, so it is easier to coordinate the drying time on the two surfaces if the cement is put on the foam first.

Flameproofing   The laws regarding flameproofing are different from state to state, but the general rule of thumb is that if a flame is held to the edge of a piece of scenery and the scenery catches fire, it is not flameproofed. If it is flameproofed it will smolder for a moment, then sputter out. The fire department has the right to come into the theatre any time they want to try this test, and if the scenery does not pass, to close the show. Scenery in shows with live fire in them (torches, candles) should be especially well flameproofed.

Oftentimes, the flameproofing will be mixed into the back paint. On other occasions it is sprayed onto the back of the scenery with a pump sprayer after it has been painted, and sometimes it is put on first, with the prime coat. To some extent this is a matter of preference but, assuming the fabric has been well sealed with the prime coat, it is better to apply flameproofing after the scene painting has been finished because it can change colors that are painted on over it. Another approach is to buy preflameproofed scenic fabric. These are a bit more expensive, but save time for the scene painters. All the major theatrical fabric supply companies stock flame retardant fabrics, as well as prebuilt flameproofed drops in standard sizes.

Recipe for Homemade Flameproofing:

1. Stir one pound each of borax and sal ammoniac into four quarts of water.

Recipe for (Gothic) Flameproofing Compound

1. Stir two pounds of flameproofing compound into one gallon of warm water. (Be careful not to put too much compound in or salt stains might result.)

PAINTS, ANILINE DYE, METALLICS   There are several types and brands of scene paint on the market. Each type is for a specific purpose, which suggests that a shop should stock a selection of at least two or three different types. The budget must be considered, of course, but there are other factors as well. Where the paint is on the set and how it is used, the intended effect the paint is supposed to produce, and the time factor (some paints take some time to prepare), must be considered as well. Many shows will require a combination of paints used on different parts of the set, because of the strengths and weaknesses of each type of paint.

Some of the brands of scene paint currently on the market are better than others. Brands that cost more are not always the best you can get. Consider what you are buying. You get more paint for your money when you buy a thick paint because you can add your own water in the shop. Check to make sure the colors are what they say they are. A few brands have odd versions of the basic colors. If burnt sienna looks maroon it will take a lot of effort to get it to look like what burnt sienna is supposed to look like. Most paint companies provide swatch books or color sample books. Send away for these and compare the colors they offer. Make sure that the paint, after it has dried, stays where it was put. If it powders off the set it can ruin costumes, not to mention the paint job.

Some paints come in paste form or, in the case of pigments, are made into paste before they are watered down into paint. To turn these into paint the paste must be broken down. *Breaking down paste* is the method by which paste is thinned into paint without creating lumps in the paint that will smear on the scenery.

To break down paste:

1. Add a very little bit of water to the paste in a bucket.
2. Stir thoroughly until all the water is mixed in.
3. Repeat the first two steps until paint is at the desired consistency.
4. As the paste gets thinner, more water can be added at a time. Be careful not to add too much at once or lumps will form.

Note: Once paint has been made you cannot just add more paste to it. If the paint is too thin, or if more is needed, break down more paste in a separate bucket, and then add the new batch to the old.

Also very important: Never mix pastes when color mixing. This will produce a most unsatisfactory streaky paint. Always break down the individual colors first, and then mix them.

Beginning scene painters have trouble deciding how thin their paint should be. Usually they lean on the thick side. Scene paint should be as thin as possible while still able to cover. At first this takes some experimentation, but eventually the scene painter learns how the right thickness of paint feels while stirring it with a mixing stick. Obviously, thinner paint can be used when painting on new fabric, but must be thicker when used on old, used fabric scenery, or on wood or foam. The thickness must ultimately be determined by the specific circumstances of the job.

Dry Pigment   Dry pigment is the oldest form of paint, going back to the cave man. It is the least expensive paint to buy, but the most expensive in terms of preparation time and effort. The best selection of colors of any paint is available in pigment form. In addition, pigment colors are the clearest and in some cases the most brilliant. Some of the colors possible in pigment form are not available in any other kind of paint.

Pigment is sold in powder form by the pound. It is usually packaged in brown paper bags. It should be stored in separate containers in a dry environment, as moisture will make it clump.

There are two ways to mix dry pigment colors, which is another aspect of them that makes them unique. The first, which is true of all paints, is to mix the individual pigments into paint form, and mix the colors wet. This, of course, involves painting test color swatches to check the way the color will look when it is dry. The second method is to mix the colors in pigment form while they are still dry. The pigment is the same color it will be after it has been made into paint, applied and dried. Its value will darken a few shades when it is wet, but will regain its original color afterwards. It is the only form of paint that can be color mixed without having to wait for test swatches to dry to get just the right color.

Any size can be used to turn pigment into paint. One of its disadvantages is that whenever such paint is thinned, it must be done with size instead of water. This makes it essential that a size barrel be kept, because great volumes of working size are needed, first to make the paint, and then to work with it. A big plastic trash can makes a good size barrel. A prominent sign should be painted on the lid that says "NOT FOR TRASH." It will be used for trash anyhow, so a strainer should be kept nearby so that cigarette butts and plastic candy wrappers will not "add texture" to the scene painting. The size in the barrel should be stirred frequently, since the glue, being heavier than the water, settles. It should be freshened every day or so, to keep the odor in the shop to a bearable minimum.

Whichever type of size is chosen to make pigment paint with should be used to thin it as well. Mixing different sizes may or may not work well. The most commonly used binder for making pigment paint is gelatine glue. However, white glue size also works well with pigments, and requires less time and effort to prepare. And it smells better.

Pigment paint has been replaced in most shops by casein paint, but many of these shops still stock pigments as well. They can be added dry to other paints to adjust colors, and sometimes they are used in paint form as an adjunct to the primary paint system in use.

Paint Recipe:

First make paste.

1. Place pigment in a bucket.

2. Slowly pour in working size, carefully stirring out lumps, until the mixture is about the consistency of toothpaste.

3. For each 1/4 gallon of paste add one tablespoon of denatured alcohol. This helps the pigment powder to dissolve in the working size.

4. Let the paste sit overnight. The pigment will have a chance to absorb the size completely, making a consistent paste. Pour a little water over the paste, but do not stir it in. This will evaporate overnight, protecting the paste underneath.

Next make paint. Only make as much paint from the paste as will be needed for each scene painting task.

5. Place the required amount of paste in a clean bucket.

6. Break down the paste with working size until it is thinned to the required consistency.

7. Add two or three tablespoons of glycerine per five gallons of paint to make the paint less brittle. Be careful not to add too much, because it retards the drying of paint. This step is optional, depending on how the paint is behaving after it has been broken down.

Casein

Casein has become a popular scene paint for many reasons. It is fairly easy to work with. It comes in a reasonably wide choice of colors. When it dries it has a flat finish that is similar to that of fresco paintings. Because stage lighting is so bright a flat finish is desirable in scene painting to keep the scenery from shining. Casein comes in paste form, so you pay for the pigment and binder, but not for the water.

When buying casein paint the scene painter should consider that some brands package more water in the paste than others, and that the price of one brand over another is not always an accurate guide to the contents of the can. Ease of application and color range should also be considered, as well as the accuracy of the colors offered.

Casein comes in one-gallon cans and, more expensively, in quart cans. Some companies offer five-gallon cans of white paste. (Save the cans to use as buckets, especially the plastic ones.) Different colors are sold on a scale of prices. White is the least expensive. The earth colors are usually sold in a moderate price range, and dye colors are the most expensive. Some companies charge the most for bright red.

To make paint the paste must be broken down. Most brands will give a paste-to-water ratio on the can, but generally these should be ignored due to the inconsistency of the thickness of the paste from color to color and the fact that different jobs require varying thicknesses of paint.

Latex   Probably the most easily available paint around that is used for scene painting is latex paint, stocked in every local paint and hardware store. It is a synthetic rubber or plastic binder based paint that comes pre-mixed in quart or gallon cans. Occasionally some colors can be found in paste form, especially white. It can be (and in many cases should be) thinned with water, and it comes in a variety of colors. Most stores do not stock a very wide choice, but will custom-mix colors from little color sample cards. As with caseins, the earth colors tend to be less expensive, and the custom-mixed colors the most expensive.

Latex forms a rubber-like seal that is fairly strong on the surface of scenery. Once the paint has set up and dried, it is easy to clean by damp mopping it. It is used to paint decks, platforms, stairs, and so on that take a lot of wear and tear from actors and dancers.

Latex comes in a choice of finishes, including gloss, semigloss and flat. In general, flat latex should be used for stage purposes.

Vinyl   Vinyl is a tough plastic-based (ethylene) paint, similar to latex. It is a very durable, flexible paint. It is sold by theatrical suppliers in quarts and gallons in a good variety of colors. It is excellent for scenery that is walked on or danced on, and will adhere to virtually any surface, including wood, masonite, fabric, and foam. It can be used out of the can, or thinned with water.

The highly saturated paint systems fall into this category, using a vinyl-acrylic base with extremely concentrated colorant. These systems allow the scene painter to choose the brilliance of the colors, from extremely bright to dull. They involve a certain amount of preparation, and tend to be a bit pricey. A neutral base is used for mixing regular colors, and a white base for pastels. Like any vinyl paint, highly saturated paints dilute with water.

Aniline Dye   Aniline dyes are used when very brilliant colors are needed. Scenery to be painted with aniline dyes should be sized first with starch and a little methacel or gum arabic to prevent the

FIGURE 3–2. Aniline dye project.
Scene painter: Linda Cappelletti.

colors from bleeding. The powdered dyes are sold by the ounce or by the pound in over thirty-five colors. Most of the colors do not mix very well with each other, but there is a wide enough selection to use them as they come. They are particularly useful for stained-glass-window effects, and for cartoon inking.

When a particularly brilliant color is wanted, the same color should be painted two or three times, allowing each coat to dry before painting the next one. This results in a more brilliant color than if one coat of thicker dye had been used.

Aniline dyes are soluble in water, in alcohol, or in oil, depending on which type you buy. For the paint shop, the type that is soluble in both oil and water, or the type that is only soluble in water should be stocked. Once a color has been made, it should be stored in a water-tight container to prevent it from crystallizing. Plastic milk containers work well for this purpose, as do glass jars.

Water Recipe:

1. Boil one quart of water.
2. Stir in one ounce of powdered aniline dye.
3. Allow to cool before using.

Bronzing Powders

Bronzing powders are used to simulate metals. They are sold by the pound in powder form, and are packaged in cans. The color range includes golds, aluminums, coppers, red, green, and blue. Realistic metallic effects can be achieved by toning with two or more bronzing powder colors. These should be mixed in small quantities, only enough for the job on hand, because they do not last very long. Margarine tubs with tight lids make excellent containers for this purpose.

Bronzing Powder Recipe:
1. Put bronzing powder in the bottom of a margarine tub, about one-quarter-inch high.
2. Slowly stir in clear gloss vinyl (or latex).
3. Keep covered when not in use.

Other Metallics There is a variety of other odd metallics including glitter, diamond dust, sequins, and so on. The best way to apply them is first to finish the conventional painting on the set piece and allow it to dry thoroughly. Spray white glue size (about one part water to seven or eight parts glue—thicker size than working size) with a mister bottle or pump sprayer. Then sprinkle the metallics on while the size is still wet. Paint stores sell a gadget called a glitter gun which does a pretty good job of sprinkling glitter evenly, once you get the hang of it.

Spray Paint Spray paint is oil-based paint in pressurized cans, available in any hardware store in a wide variety of colors and brands. It is used for small jobs in scene painting, including painting props and blacking out wires used for flying scenery. It is not great for the atmosphere of the shop (or the world), or the lungs, and it should be used only in well-ventilated areas. If there are air currents in the work space the scene painter should remain up-wind of the work.

Realistic metallic objects can be achieved by toning them with light blends of different shades of the same basic color of spray paint (like gold and bronze). This type of toning works well on other objects too, such as streetlight poles, metal railings, statues, and the like. Flat black spray paint is used to black out hanging hardware and wires, and when very lightly sprayed makes good soot around a fireplace, chimney, or boiler.

Spray paint also works well through stencils of lettering or ornament. Using screen, scrim, erosion cloth, or other such materials as stencils can provide very interesting painted textures on a set.

Clear Finish Various clear finishes are used to simulate the sheen of varnished wood, tile in floors or fireplaces, slate, and any shiny surface on the set or on furniture. Shellac, varnish, and polyurethane used to be the only choices available, but now there are water-soluble clear vinyls and clear latexes sold in gloss, semi-gloss, and flat finishes. These are easy to use and clean up, and provide a lot of control over the shininess of the gloss.

Clear flat can be brushed or sprayed onto scenery. It is white in the can, but dries clear. It should be slightly watered down before using it, and puddling should be avoided. A couple of thin coats of clear flat will give the appearance of a shine to a floor without making it too reflective. When used judiciously clear flat can help painted tiles to look real if it is dry brushed over each "tile" in a different direction. It is also used as a sealer against stage blood and other liquid props. Once clear vinyl or latex has dried overnight, it can be safely damp mopped, or even lightly scrubbed.

Clear gloss should be used only on relatively small areas for effect. Door, window, and arch molding can be made to stand out from set walls if they are glossed. Sometimes it is better, however, to use semi-gloss instead to give the impression of high gloss without creating strong reflections.

Glaze   Glaze is simply very thin paint. It is so thin that colors painted underneath it can be seen through it. It is applied to scenery with a brush or with a sprayer. Size is added to pigment paint, or water is added to premixed paints to make glaze. It is excellent for painting shadows and for toning. If scenery has come out brighter than expected a thin glaze can help to tone it down.

4
Preparing to paint

PAINTING SURFACES

Before the scene painter begins to paint, a decision must be made about the surface to be painted on. In general this decision is based on two factors: what materials have the most appropriate qualities for the particular desired effect, and the budget.

Scenery provides an environment in which dramatic action takes place, but it should not be a scene stealer. Under the usually bright stage lights a nontextured surface seems to glare. Such a glare attracts the eye, and distracts from the main action of the play, usually having something to do with the actors, who, in general, do not glare (except the villains). Therefore, textured surfaces are preferred, because they disperse light and reflect it evenly. Oftentimes a textile fabric will be chosen because the weave of the fiber provides a desirable texture. Flats, backdrops, and even floors are covered with fabric to provide an even surface that helps to reduce the glare. The fabric also must take paint well, and each has its own characteristics that affect these considerations.

The correct fabric choice is important to the final look of the scenery. There is no rule of thumb that flats, for example, are always covered with canvas or muslin. This might be appropriate for the walls of the Manningham parlor in *Angel Street*, but out of place on the factory walls in *R.U.R.*, where a glossier look might be entirely appropriate.

The scenic artist should be familiar with many materials and the way paint takes to their surfaces. When a small budget precludes the use of an ideal material or fabric, there are usually less costly alternatives which, although they will not be able to provide the desired effect to its fullest potential, will at least suggest the visual qualities of the more expensive choice.

Canvas Canvas duck is made from cotton or linen. It comes unbleached, bleached, or dyed, and can be bought natural or flameproofed. It is the most preferred material for covering flats, for opaque drops, wings, borders, and ground cloths. Eight-ounce cotton duck is most often purchased for stage use, because linen is very expensive. Its strength and the weave of the fabric make it a good choice, as well as the fact that it takes paints well. It can be obtained in a variety of widths up to one-hundred-twenty inches. It is sold by the yard, or by the bolt (about 50 yards).

Muslin Muslin is a lighter weight fabric than canvas, and has a finer weave. This means that it tears more easily (of course, at the least opportune moment), and its refractive quality is less effective. Nevertheless, many theatre shops use muslin, because it is less expensive than canvas. It comes in heavy, medium, and light weight. Although heavy-weight muslin has the strongest and coarsest weave, many theatres use medium-weight muslin because of the price difference. Light-weight muslin is impractical for use on scenery. It tears very easily at the slightest provocation.

Muslin, like canvas, comes bleached, unbleached, or dyed, flameproofed or natural. Generally, unbleached muslin is used for flats and backdrops. Sometimes bleached or blue-dyed muslin is used to construct sky backings, drops and cycloramas.

Muslin is too light weight a fabric to use for ground cloths (although, on a tight budget a ground cloth made from old muslin that has been painted four or five times will hold up for short runs if the show does not contain too much violent action or dancing). However, it is preferred for translucent drops because the lighter weight fabric allows light to pass through more readily. When painting a translucency, the seams have to be disguised in the painting. If this is impossible, seamless full-sized drops can be ordered from theatrical fabric suppliers. This is expensive, though.

Wood Large areas of bare wood do not often appear on scenery unless the theatre is restricted to a very low budget. In normal use it appears in cornices, floor moulding, chair rails, doors, windows, arches, and in furniture. In these guises it is often painted or finished with a clear finish to make it seem more glossy than the walls, floor, ceiling, and so on. Since wood (or good wood) is relatively smooth, it is naturally glossier than textile fabrics. One method of reducing this quality (which also works on flats that have been painted so often that the weave of the fabric has been filled in) is scumbling with thick paint, which will, by virtue of the randomly crossed brush strokes, break up the evenness of the surface. Using a flat-finish paint instead of a gloss also helps.

If the paint is mixed too thin, the grain of the wood will assert itself. This can be an asset under controlled circumstances, but more often it is a liability. It is best to test a small area to see how well the paint covers it, and then to thicken the paint if necessary.

Masonite In general, masonite is a difficult surface to scene paint on. It is even smoother than wood, and if the paint is not thick enough it will not cover, and will smear unevenly. Masonite has some important advantages to construction, however, and should be covered with canvas or muslin before painting, if possible. It is sometimes used for reveals or facings, especially those that curve and must be strong. Sometimes it is used to cover the deck when the wooden stage floor underneath is splintered or old. It provides a floor surface that is uniform, and masonite does not splinter (although sometimes it warps). Masonite has a smooth surface on one side and a mottled one on the other. If it is not to be covered by some other material the smooth side should always be used. The mottled side drinks paint, and is very difficult to cover.

Easy Curve Easy curve is thin Upson board that curves easily around round scenery forms or armatures. It is often used for facings and curved reveals. The type that has one mottled surface should be used, and this textured surface should be painted upon. As a surface for paint it is preferable to masonite, but, being a flimsier material, it is more likely to succumb to an ill-aimed foot or a clumsy ingenue.

Easy curve and masonite come in four-foot by eight-foot sheets. In some areas easy curve is hard to find, since many lumber yards do not carry it, but it is worth ordering if time allows.

Velour Twenty- or twenty-five-ounce cotton velour is commonly used for stage curtains, and can also be used for painted set pieces. It has a very deep pile that gives it a rich appearance. Cut-outs, flats, and drops, skillfully painted on velour appear convincingly three-dimensional. The thick nap makes velour more difficult to paint than canvas, because it absorbs a lot more paint, but the results are well worth the effort. Velour is available by the yard, or in bolts up to fifty-four inches wide, and in a wide variety of colors.

Duvetyn Duvetyn is another cotton material which is used when velour is beyond the budget. Its nap is less rich and even than that of velour. It can be purchased by the yard or in bolts thirty-six or fifty-four inches wide.

Gauzes   There are several different gauzes that are used in the theatre. Gauzes give scenery a light, airy look. A scene painted on a gauze will be perceived by the audience just as a scene on a conventional drop would be when it is lit from the front (assuming a gauze with a relatively small, even open, weave, such as scrim). When an actor, a prop, or other scenery is lit behind the painted gauze the scene painted on its front disappears to reveal whatever is behind it. Sometimes draped gauzes are used in scenery. When lit through they give a light, magical effect. An underwater scene is an example of a possibly effective use of draped gauze. Finally, gauzes are used to provide texture to wood or carved foam scenery. It is applied with size and smoothed on to create an even texture, or crinkled on to provide a rough one.

Sharkstooth scrim is a very good quality gauze with a square-patterned weave that is even across large areas. It comes in bolts thirty feet wide, although with tenacity a supplier can be found who is willing to sell smaller pieces. It can be purchased in natural form, bleached, or dyed, and it is available factory flameproofed. It is somewhat expensive, but is a choice material.

Cotton scrim is sold at a lower price, but in smaller widths, up to fifty-eight inches.

Theatrical gauze is a linen scrim with a simpler weave than that of sharkstooth scrim. It is available in widths of up to seventy-two inches.

Filled scrim is a scrim on which the weave has been filled in, leaving the texture of the gauze, without having the weave open. It is a useful textural material, especially in a scene (such as a dream sequence) where a part of the set must become transparent. By using filled scrim to cover the rest of the set, there is no discrepancy of texture to alert the audience that part of the set will become transparent until the proper moment arrives.

Bobbinet is a lightweight gauze with a hexagonal weave. Translucent scenery can be painted on bobbinet, giving the scene an ethereal appearance. It comes in widths up to thirty-one feet.

Cheesecloth is a very loose weave gauze. It is too flimsy to use by itself, but makes a good texturing material on props and foam units. It is available in fabric stores and surgical supply stores, or in small quantities in grocery and hardware stores.

Burlap is a heavier fabric made of jute. It has a loose, uneven weave, often with thick spots appearing randomly in the fiber. In natural form it is tan colored, but is available in a variety of colors. It comes in several choices of width, up to seventy-two inches, and may be purchased factory flameproofed.

Erosion cloth is a heavy jute gauze with an uneven, open weave. It is very rough, appearing to be some sort of magnified burlap. It can be hung as a drop, or applied to a surface to provide a coarse texture. It is manufactured for the purpose of laying over yards or fields to prevent soil erosion, so it is available at plant nurseries.

Monk's Cloth

Monk's cloth is a medium-heavy fabric with an even but loose weave. The looseness of the weave allows individual strands to be removed to create frayed edges. It is a cotton fabric, and is available natural or flameproofed in forty-eight-inch width.

Felt

Felt is made by compressing fibers together instead of weaving them. It does not actually have a nap, but it is fuzzy and therefore, a poor man's answer to velour when the budget will not even allow for duvetyn. The results of painting on felt are nowhere near as satisfactory as they would be on velour or duvetyn, but still approach the general look.

Felt is more often used for making props. When treated with paints and other materials felt can be molded, shaped, distressed, and so on to look like all manner of different things. For instance, when rubbed with soap and paint it can be used to simulate leather.

Felt comes in many colors, flame retardant or natural, in widths up to seventy-two inches.

PREPARING THE MATERIAL

Before painting begins it is important to prepare each set piece properly. If time is taken beforehand to prepare the surface, it will insure some ease of application of the paint, and that the scenery will look right when it gets on stage. Sometimes, in the rush of production it seems as if it would save time to skip steps in the preparation. When that happens it usually turns out that more time is spent repairing problems that would not have occurred if it had been prepared right in the first place. For instance, if a translucent drop is not sealed on both sides before the back is painted, paint is likely to seep through the drop where thin paint on the front will not be able to cover it. Uneven blobs are unnecessarily caused.

It is wiser to plan all the necessary steps into the painting schedule. When flats are being sized, back-painted, or whatever, the drying time should be used to mix colors for later use, touch up furniture, paint mouldings, and so on, so there will not be big gaps in the day when the crew has nothing to do.

Covering Flats

Usually flats are covered by the carpentry shop crew as part of the construction process. It is important for the scene painter to have some knowledge of this, however, because the flat-covering process can directly effect the painting process.

On hard covered flats the fabric is glued onto the plywood. The glue mixture is spread out evenly onto the wood, and the fabric is brushed on over it. On soft covered flats the edges of the fabric are glued onto the stiles and rails of the frame (not the toggles!). In both cases it is important to the painter that a diluted glue mixture is used.

White glue is the adhesive most often used to cover flats. When used at its full strength it dries hard and leaves shiny marks on the fabric. Sometimes paint can be repelled by the hardened glue, causing uneven coverage and streaking. The same paint will always look different when applied to different surfaces, and when full-strength glue is used it changes the surface characteristics of the fabric where it has been applied. The paint on the glue areas will show up as marks on an otherwise even coat of paint.

The answer to this difficulty is to water down the glue. A one-to-one ratio of glue and water is sufficient to preserve the integrity of the fabric surface while still retaining enough strength to adhere the fabric to the wood.

Some technicians prefer to staple the fabric to the flat to hold it in place while the glue is drying. These staples should be removed as soon as possible. Canvas and muslin shrink when they are wet, and even the glue/water mixture will cause the fabric to shrink. The staples hold the fabric in place, and puckers form around them as the fabric shrinks. These will be permanent when the glue dries. This, of course, causes an inconsistency in the surface texture that will probably show up when the set is lit on stage.

Dutchmans are sometimes applied by the construction crew, and sometimes by the paint crew. If applied by the construction crew, chances are the dutchman will be put on with a glue/water mixture. The same mixture should be used that was used to adhere the fabric to the frames. The dutchman should be a single strip of the same covering fabric used on the flats, four to six inches wide. The dutchman is dipped into a bucket of glue/water mixture until it is soaked, then wrung out between two fingers. It is then placed over the crack to be covered, and patted smooth with the fingers, or brushed on with a glue brush. The fabric tends to curl at the edges, forming a raised, hard edge on each side of the dutchman if allowed to dry that way. These edges should be carefully uncurled and feathered out with a brush to form the most inconspicuous edge possible. It is also helpful for the grain of the dutchman to match the direction of the grain of the covering fabric.

When the paint crew applies a dutchman it can be done during the process of applying a base coat. The dutchman is dipped into the base color, then applied to the flats in the same manner it would be using a glue/water mixture. The binder in the paint should be sufficient to hold the dutchman in place. If it is not, more binder can be added to a bucket of the same color paint.

Where to Paint

The decision to paint scenery up or down is usually dictated by convenience or necessity. If a shop is equipped with a paint frame it will likely be chosen for drops and flats. The scene painter remains on the floor with all the paint and tools handy while the set rises and descends at the painter's convenience. A good deal of floor space is saved by using a paint frame, and the scene painter can easily back up to view the work in progress from a distance.

On the other hand, two scene painters can grid a drop on the floor a lot faster than on the frame, and paint does not drip down the drop. Although air circulation needed for drying is better around a frame, decreasing the drying time a bit, special triangular wooden frames can be constructed to lift the sides of a drop from the floor, and air can then be circulated underneath with large fans.

If space allows, the drop should be painted all at once. Painting half of the drop in a restricted space, then folding it over to paint the other half is a difficult prospect. It is hard to match the two halves. Not only are lines likely to waver in the center, but no matter how well the scene painter remembers or has recorded the techniques used on the first half, it is very difficult to duplicate them on the second half. Paint frames that are smaller than a full stage drop have their uses, but it is wise to avoid painting a full stage drop on one if there is sufficient floor space elsewhere in the shop.

Tacking Scenery on the Floor

The first step when tacking scenery on the shop floor is to clean the floor, especially if the paint area is shared with the construction crew. Anything lying under a drop will show up in the painting. The floor should be thoroughly swept at least three times, and then wet-mopped if necessary. There is nothing more aggravating than having some old paint, dye, stage blood, or other unwanted substance seep up through a new clean drop.

Next, absorbent paper, such as heavy-weight Kraft paper, should be laid out neatly over the work area. This can be stapled down at the ends to keep it from sailing all over the shop when the drop creates air currents as it is unfurled.

When the floor is ready, the drop can be unfolded and

laid, front side up (unless there is a special reason why the back should be treated first), loosely on the floor. A chalk line should be snapped where the top of the drop will lie. The center of this line should be measured and marked. The center of the drop should have been marked on its webbing when it was constructed. If it has not been done it should be measured and marked at this stage (the drop should be halved carefully and the center of the bottom should be found as well). The mark on the webbing should be lined up with the center point on the chalk line, and the drop can be stapled at this point, through the webbing.

Next, the drop should be stretched along the top. One side of the top of the drop should be stapled along the line from the center out, until the corner is reached. The same process should be repeated on the other side. Tacking down the drop this way allows it to lie naturally, avoiding wrinkles that might be caused by uneven stretching. Staples should be placed about every four inches to minimize puckering of the fabric when the drop is wet.

The center of the bottom of the drop should be stretched away from the center top, as far as it will go without stretching it. The distance from top center to bottom center is measured. This measurement should be taken from the top left corner down, and from the top right corner down. A line should be snapped between these points, right and left.

Now the bottom center point on the drop should be lined up and stapled to the bottom center point on the new chalk line. It is vital that the center line formed between the top and bottom center points be perpendicular to the original chalk line at the top of the drop. If this is not the case all the vertical lines on the drop will become diagonal ones when it is hung up. The bottom of the drop is then stapled to its chalk line the same way the top was done. From center, the drop should be stretched gently downward as it is stapled toward each side. If the drop was constructed with a pipe pocket it should be smoothed out underneath the drop when the bottom is being stapled down, so it will not create unwanted marks when the drop is painted.

Finally, the sides can be stapled down. Again, the center of each side is found, and staples are put in from center to top and bottom. The sides should be stretched out a bit, but horizontally only. If stretched vertically, a wrinkle of fabric will collect at the top or bottom, present difficulties during the painting, and cause the drop to hang unevenly.

When stapling down a drop only hand staplers should be used. Pneumatic staple guns push staples into the floor too efficiently for this operation. Most hand staple guns will not push the staple all the way down, leaving the top sticking up sufficiently to grab it with pliers or pry it up with a screwdriver when the drop is taken up. A drop should never be pulled on to get staples out of the floor. Often the fabric will tear along its weave, ruining the finished drop.

Staples should be placed parallel one-half inch to an inch from the edge of the fabric so that enough fabric is held down to prevent the drop from ripping off the staples when it shrinks. When the drop is sized all the fabric should be covered, but when it is painted the bottom line of the painting should be planned to end about an inch above the staples. When the drop is taken up this edge can be trimmed along a line snapped across the bottom to remove the puckers caused by the drop shrinking against the staples.

Stapling a scrim to the floor requires much the same process, but a good deal more care. Again, the floor is cleaned thoroughly. Mopping is unnecessary because the floor will be covered with a water repellant material that prevents anything from soaking through it. Wax paper or polyethylene sheeting should be carefully laid out and tacked down for this purpose.

Stretching scrim is a delicate operation, because the loose weave of the material pulls more easily than that of a more conventional fabric. It is important to stretch the fabric evenly without distorting it. It is easy to see when the grain of the weave is being distorted, and care must be taken to compensate by stretching from the opposite direction when it does.

Scrim tends to stretch out when it is painted, and for this reason, if it is to be framed, it should be painted before it is stretched onto its frame. Furthermore, if it is to be painted up it should be backed by a flat surface like plywood or masonite. The pressure of a brush on an unbacked piece of gauze is sufficient to distort the fabric, causing puckers and dents.

Tacking Scenery onto the Paint Frame

Tacking a drop onto a paint frame is a somewhat simpler proposition, because gravity is used to make sure the drop will hang straight. (We assume the paint frame has been installed level. It should be checked.) Drops should be hung from the top of the frame which provides a straight, horizontal starting point. Several long pieces of 2 by 4 should be kept near the paint frame for tacking up drops. The frame is lowered so the top can be comfortably reached. A 2-by-4 batten is pieced along the top edge of the frame. The center point should be found and marked on the batten.

The floor near the frame slot should be swept clean, and it should be dry. A sheet or two of Kraft paper should be laid out in front of the slot to help keep the drop clean while it is being fastened to the frame.

Now the drop is unfolded and heaped onto the floor before the frame. The top corners are temporarily stapled to the ends of the battens (as far as the corners will reach). Three or four staples on each side, about four inches apart, should be enough to hold the drop up. This is done through the webbing to prevent tearing.

The center point on the webbing is matched with the center point on the batten. The center is stapled, lining the top of the webbing up with the top of the batten. The webbing is smoothed out along the batten from center, and stapled about every four inches to each side. When the ends are reached, the temporary staples are removed and the webbing is smoothed out on the ends and restapled to the corners. (It will be found that extra fabric ends up between the temporary staples and the ones put in from center. This is caused by the weight of the drop pulling down when originally hung up by the corners. The drop is hung this way to make it easier to staple it up from center, without the hinderance of fighting its weight while trying to line it up evenly.)

Now the frame is raised with two assistants carefully unfurling the drop from each side as it rises. The drop should hang naturally. (If it does not check how straight the top batten has been put on. If it is straight, the drop may have been faultily constructed.) Another 2 by 4 batten is located at the bottom of the drop. Its location should be measured right and left from the corners of the top batten to make sure the lower one is nailed on parallel to the top one. Since the drop is hanging up it is not necessary to find the exact center point along the bottom. The approximate center is stapled to the batten where it falls across it, slightly stretching downwards. The bottom is then smoothed along the batten from center to each side, gently stretching downward, and stapled along the way the top was put on.

Vertical battens are now nailed to the frame along the sides of the drop. Starting about halfway up, the drop is stretched gently to the side and stapled to the batten (staples should always be placed parallel to the side of the fabric to minimize the possibility that it might pull off the batten). Staples are now put in about every four inches up and down the sides, stretching horizontally only. (Vertical stretching will cause the material to pucker at the top or bottom, and should be carefully avoided.)

When flats are tacked to the paint frame they should be securely fastened on with duplex nails. The frame should be

lowered so that a row of flats can be nailed along the top of
the frame. Flats will usually stay on well enough with three or
four well-placed nails, but if a flat should flop or bend away
from the frame, more should be used. The flat should be even
with the frame. If the bottom sticks forward it is likely to
catch on the edge of the frame slot with sometimes rather
spectacular results. The flat can only bend so far before the
pressure of the descending frame explodes it, leaving shards of
wood dangling from the canvas.

Flats should be put on the frame in the order in which
they are lined up on the painter's elevation. This way it is easy
for the painter to keep track of the logic of the set, and any
toning or patterning (such as wallpaper) will make sense as it is
being painted. Because flats are sometimes built shorter than
the full height of the set so they can rest on platform levels,
their bottoms are not always at the same height. The tops, however, are almost always even. The tops of the flats should, therefore, be hung even with each other. If there is room on the
frame for a second row of flats beneath the top row, a horizontal line should be projected about six inches below the lowest
bottom of the top row, by stretching a piece of string horizontally across the frame. The tops of the flats in this second row
are lined up with the string. If possible the lowest row of flats
should be about three feet from the bottom trough of the
frame. This precaution will avoid the necessity of kneeling to
paint the bottom of the set, and will prevent any debris that has
collected in the trough from mixing with the paint onto the
flats.

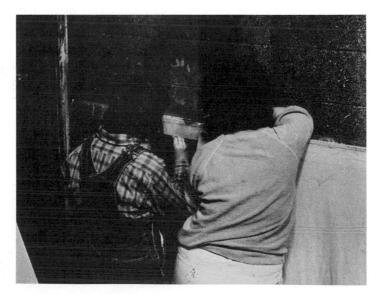

FIGURE 4–1. Battens are placed on the paint frame, and a drop is stretched onto the frame.

FIRST COATS

Once the scenery has been tacked down it must be stretched and sealed. This is accomplished by priming the canvas or muslin on the set pieces. The *prime coat* is brushed evenly onto the fabric. It is composed of glue and water which has been mixed in the proper proportions to make working size. Sometimes Danish whiting is added to the size to give the fabric extra body. Since size has no color to it, it is difficult to see where it has been brushed on, and small holidays (bits of canvas accidentally left unpainted) are particularly difficult to find. For this reason a little paint or pigment can be added to the size so it can be seen on the white fabric. It is important that there be no holidays in the prime coat because they will cause puckers in the fabric. Holidays in the prime coat remain dry so they do not stretch with the rest of the drop, and these breaks in the sealing of the fabric allow back paint to seep through, as well as causing uneven coverage in the base coat.

Experimentation will show why sizing scenery is worthwhile in the preparation of scenic fabric. If a drop is not sized, the base coat will stretch it but probably will not seal it well. A twenty-by-forty-foot drop will take about eight to ten gallons of paint for an overall base coat. If the drop has been sized it needs only five or so gallons to cover it. This represents a substantial savings in the cost of paint, because size costs only a fraction of what paint costs.

The next coat is the *base coat*. This is usually a single base color that will be used as the undercolor for the painted set piece. Sometimes more than one color is used. In a woodland scene, for instance, the top (sky) might be based a light blue, the center (woods) a green, and the bottom (ground) brown. Occasionally, such a coat will be sprayed on with a pump spray-

FIGURE 4–2. The drop is sized using priming brushes. A little pigment has been added to the size so the painters can see which areas they have covered.

76

er, toning the undercolors with sprays, but letting the natural white of the fabric come through to produce an airy, spacious effect. Care should be taken not to mix the base color to read too brilliantly. It is wise to mix all the main colors and try to test patch on a special flat to make sure all the color relationships are right before committing gallons of paint to the base coat on the scenery.

When the base color is satisfactory it is applied to the scenery with priming brushes. If the scenery is on the floor, the brushes are taped to the ends of bamboo brush extenders so the painter may stand while base coating and paint with a sweeping movement. Care must be taken to avoid holidays, which will show up as bright white patches. If the paint is thin enough, the choice of brush strokes will not matter because the paint will be too thin to obliterate the fabric weave. This is the most desirable approach because, after all, it is why fabric is used in the first place.

When base coating an old drop or flats that have developed elephant hide (canvas with so many coats of paint that it is smooth, thick and scaly), a brush stroke resembling an "x" is used. The paint is mixed thicker to cover old scenery, and the "x" strokes will create something of a texture that will serve the same purpose, though not necessarily as well, as the texture of a fabric's weave. Theoretically, a drop or flat should not be painted more than two or three times at the most, but the realities of today's Arts budgets demand more recycling in some theatres. Some stock theatres get ten or more shows out of a single drop before it is put out to pasture. By this time the drop is usually cracked and peeling. Chips one-eighth-inch thick fall off of it. Realistically, it cannot be rolled or tripped. But patches of the current show cling tenaciously to older layers of paint throughout the show's run.

Backpainting is another important step in the preparation of scenery, especially soft scenery. It helps to opaque the fabric scenery so that unwanted light will not come through, spoiling the illusion of solid walls. It also prevents light from reflecting off white scenery backs onto other scenery such as sky backings.

Some scene painters backpaint after the painting on the front has been finished. If the scenery has been properly sealed in the prime coat, and if the backpainting is applied carefully, this method works fine. The scene painter must be careful that the flat or drop is not leaning against anything, because contact with a hard object through the fabric will cause paint to seep through to the front. Relatively thick black or dark gray paint is used since it effectively screens out light.

Other scene painters prefer to backpaint before the scenery on the front is painted on (but after the prime coat). This way, if there is seepage through the fabric, the base coat will cover it, and no repairs to the finished scenery need be feared. Less care is necessary, and if inexperienced painters are assigned to this operation this second method is preferred.

This is the point where the flame retardant is applied. It can be applied in a separate coat, or it can be broken down and added to the backpaint.

Another use for backpainting is for selectively blacking out the backs of translucent drops. There are many possible uses for *translucencies*. One example is in the creation of a sunset using a combination of painted scenery and stage lighting. The drop is sized with starch on the front and back sides. Clouds that will change color are laid out in the same location on the front and back of the drop, while the rest of the scene is only laid out on the front. Care must be taken that the clouds do not fall across seams in the drop. The back of the drop is backpainted to black out only those areas where the designated clouds will not be. These clouds are then painted on the back with analine dyes or thin paint. (Dyes provide more brilliant colors that are very effective when used in this technique.) The drop is taken up and retacked with the front side up. The full scene is painted on the drop in thin paint, the clouds painted white and fluffy as they would be seen by day.

When the drop is lit normally from the front the daylight scene is viewed like any normal painted drop. Backlight from an electric lowered behind the drop is aimed at the general area of the backpainted clouds. As the backlight is brightened and the front light gradually dimmed, the clouds seem to change color. Colors in the backlights can add variety to the effect. Skillful manipulation of the lights on a well-painted translucency can create a convincing spectacle.

LAYING OUT A DROP

There are three primary techniques for laying out a drop. This is the point in scene painting where the scaled painter's elevations are blown up to full size. It is important that the scene painter maintain the scale relationship between the elevation and the scenery, because carelessness at this point can severely distort the proportions of the set.

The first method is used on relatively uncomplicated and loosely drawn designs. This involves freehand drawing, using measured reference points. The center line is found on the elevation, and snapped in charcoal on the drop. Do not use chalk, because it will not come off! The important reference points are measured from the bottom of the elevation, top to bottom, and from the center line, right to left. These distances are scaled up and marked in charcoal on the drop. (Example: If the elevation is in 1/2-inch-equals-one-foot scale, three inches on the elevation equal six feet on the drop.) The scenic artist draws freehand the appropriate cartooning, using a drawing stick and charcoal, and making sure the lines go through the correct reference points. Incorrect lines are whipped off the fabric with a flog (taking care that the scenery is not beaten with the wooden handle, which might tear it). When drawing is completed, the scenic artist steps back to check the work against the elevation for scale and proportion. When it is correct the drawing is inked in with a marker, and the entire drop is then flogged to remove all the excess charcoal. (Charcoal left on the work tends to mix with the paint, changing colors and streaking.)

The second method uses a grid technique to blow up the scene. The size of the grid depends on the complexity of the drawing. Smaller squares are used for more intricate designs. Using a 1/2-inch-equals-one-foot elevation as an example, acetate is taped over the elevation to protect it, and a grid of one-half-inch squares is drawn over it. Using charcoal lines a one-foot-square grid is then snapped onto the drop. Each grid line on the elevation is numbered along the bottom and assigned a letter along the sides. The corresponding lines on the drop are similarly labeled. The drawing is then transferred square by square onto the drop, using a drawing stick. When the drawing on all the squares has been transferred, the drawing is checked by stepping back to get an overall view. Often lines that cross grid lines kink at the grid, because they have been treated as segments instead of whole lines. These are now smoothed out using sweeping strokes of the drawing stick. When the drawing is complete and correct, it is inked in, and the charcoal, including the grid, is flogged off.

FIGURE 4–3. A scaled grid is drawn onto the drop. Charcoal marks are measured down the sides of the drop every twelve inches. Two scene painters snap the horizontal lines with a snap line filled with powdered charcoal.

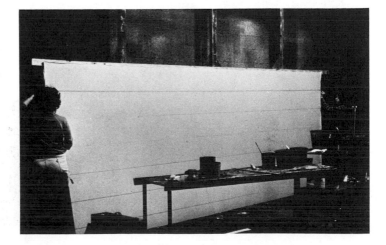

FIGURE 4–4. Charcoal marks are measured along the top and bottom of the drop every twelve inches. A scene painter snaps horizontal grid lines with a bow snap line.

FIGURE 4–5. Using the grid, the drawing is applied square by square.

FIGURE 4–6. Mistakes in the drawing are flogged out.

FIGURE 4–7. The drawing is finished and corrected, and inked in with a marker. The grid is then flogged out.

Finally, when laying out a very complicated design that must be very exact, an overhead projector, slide projector, or opaque projector is used. The design is projected directly onto the drop, and the lines are traced with a waterproof marker.

5

Basic techniques

Scene painting is a giant version of painting scale models or painter's elevations. Most of the techniques are the same, except for the difference in scale. Good scene painters are often also good at painting elevations. It would make sense, if it were possible, to get giants to do our scene painting for us, as though they were painting scaled elevations. Since there are no giant scene painters around we must do it ourselves, but for purposes of scale it is useful to keep our giant painter in mind. His wrist would be the size of a normal person's forearm, and his forearm the size of a whole normal-sized arm.

On a painter's elevation a two-foot line is represented as only two inches, and can be drawn by anchoring the hand at the wrist, and then turning the wrist with brush in hand. By the same token, a five-inch line is drawn by anchoring the elbow, and moving the entire hand along the line as it is painted. When you blow this scale up to our giant's size you need the same leverage to get steady, unbroken lines. Working from the wrist will produce small, unreadable lines that are useless in the larger scale, especially when painting for a larger theatre. A sensible solution is to incapacitate the wrist by grasping the brush like a hammer instead of between the forefinger middle finger, and thumb as one would hold a pen. This forces the painter to paint larger strokes from the elbow (the giant's wrist) or from the shoulder (the giant's forearm).

The question of scale is very important. The giant, by the nature of his size, would naturally see the scenery from a fair vantage point, but a human scene painter must constantly back up in order to see the whole piece of scenery and how well it is working visually. A lot of brush strokes might look perfectly dreadful close up, but read entirely differently, or not at all, from a distance.

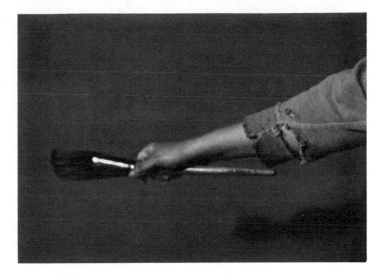

FIGURE 5–1. Holding a brush
for maximum leverage.

The basic techniques used for scene painting seem rough from a near perspective. A common shop scene is when a first-time scene painter looks on in horror as a more experienced one spatters what seems to be a perfectly finished piece of scenery that has taken hours to "complete." Yet, from the giant's point of view (and that of the distant audience), the same spatter is similar to the little dots that makes up pictures in books and magazines. They aren't perceived as dots at all, but as a smooth texture that helps make up a picture.

The term *texture technique* does not actually refer to three-dimensional objects. It describes the techniques used in scene painting to simulate texture in two dimensions. These techniques are methods of quickly applying various painted textures over large areas of scenery, making the flat surface seem richer, less flat, and more interesting to the eye. This is achieved by using the brush in a number of ways, or by simply using textured tools like sponges or rags to apply the paint. Most of these tools, including brushes, can be used in several different ways, and experimentation will suggest many different textural effects that can be achieved with each tool. Dragging the edge of a roller, for example, will produce a soft, broken line. Stippling with it at random angles produces a texture of rectangular shapes. Of course, rolling it will produce a broad, even line. There is no scene painting tool that is limited to only one type of application, and this greatly widens the range of effects it is possible to achieve.

The texture techniques include scumbling, blending, spattering and spraying, stippling, dry brushing, rag rolling, feather dusting, sponging, and stamping. These, along with lining, are the building blocks of scene painting technique. They are used alone or in combination to create more complicated effects, and to simulate objects or materials.

Before trying a technique on the actual scenery it is important, especially for beginning scene painters, to try it out on a test area first. This only takes a moment, and it resolves some of the problems that need to be worked out without spoiling the actual set. This allows the scene painter to become used to a particular tool, method of use and the thickness of the paint, and how these elements work together. For example, spattering should always be started to one side of the work each time the brush is dipped in paint to make sure the paint is coming off the brush in the right quantity and consistency. It is even a good idea to try a test when lining to see how long a line can be painted before the brush has to be dipped again in the paint.

Lining

Painting lines on scenery is called *lining*. This is done with liners, either free-hand, or with a straightedge. Liners come in different widths for painting thick or thin lines, and full advantage should be taken of this fact. It is also possible to paint thinner lines with thicker brushes by holding the brush on edge, but it is usually a better choice to use a smaller brush for thin lines. If the brush is well trained (the shape of the bristle bundle maintained), lines of consistent thickness can be made with them without having to deal with inadvertently changing the angle the scene painter is holding the brush at. Thus, one-half-inch lines are painted with a one-half-inch liner, one-inch lines with a one-inch liner, and so on. It is a bad idea to create thicker lines with multiple strokes of a thinner brush, because it is virtually impossible to control the actual line thickness. It is better to use the right brush in the first place. Doing it right saves having to do it again.

It takes a steady hand and the ability to adjust the pressure on the brush (less pressure at first when the brush is full of paint, and progressively more as the paint is used up) to get a consistent line over a distance of several feet. It is well worth developing this skill, because it will result in better looking, slicker painting.

Lining with a straightedge is a simple task, although it is a little easier when painting down, because it is easier to prevent the straightedge from slipping. It is important to hold the brush at a ninety-degree angle to the straightedge so the bristles only touch the scenery, and not the beveled bottom of the wood. This prevents the paint from seeping under the straightedge, and making a mess. Every so often the bottom of the straightedge should be wiped or allowed to dry.

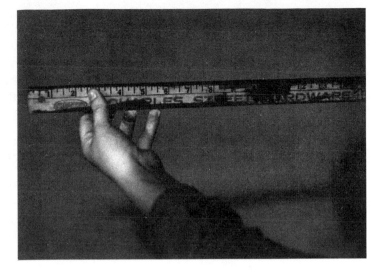

FIGURE 5–2. Holding a yardstick. The forefinger and middle finger space the yardstick from the scenery. The other end of the yardstick is held against it.

When painting up, wooden yardsticks are commonly used because they are very light weight and easy to hold in place. A yardstick should be held in one hand, leaving the other free to paint with. It is balanced from one end, holding the other end against the scenery to anchor it. The end the hand is holding is held away from the scenery by using one finger as a spacer, so the yardstick actually touches the scenery only at one end. This is done for the same reason that straightedges are beveled—to keep paint from seeping behind the wood onto the scenery. The brush is held at a ninety-degree angle to the yardstick, and the line is painted.

The yardstick should be held between the thumb, the index finger and the middle finger, with the index finger acting as a spacer to keep the wood off the canvas. The ring finger and little finger support it from underneath to insure that the pressure of the brush above the yard stick will not force it down in the middle of painting a line.

All straight lines should be painted using a straight edge of some kind. Since the arm attaches at a pivot point at the shoulder, it wants to act as a compass, naturally creating an arc. Thus, what may seem like a straight line during the execution frequently turns out to be curved when the scene painter steps back to view it. Straightedges also prevent wavy lines, which can be especially disturbing when the line is supposed to represent the edge of an object, or the shadow of a straight-edged object.

Scene painters should cultivate not only a steady hand, but a steady arm for freehand lining. Again, it is important to take advantage of the natural leverage provided from the elbow and the shoulder. Painting in this large a scale can require the

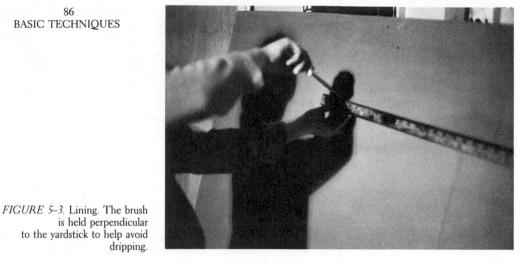

FIGURE 5–3. Lining. The brush is held perpendicular to the yardstick to help avoid dripping.

use of the whole body for long brush strokes. When using a brush extender, the entire apparatus should become an extension of the arm. Very long, consistent lines are possible when the motion of the brush originates at the shoulder. This creates the movement of what amounts to a five-foot-long arm.

Cartooning is lining that is used to outline objects. This is usually done with a liner, although an ink marker can be used. Here, again, it is essential to create consistent lines that will clearly define the objects being drawn.

FIGURE 5–4. Cartooning. Simple cartooning accomplished with a liner.

FIGURE 5–5. Dry brushing

FIGURE 5–6. Dry scumble

Dry Brushing *Dry brushing* is used for creating a lot of different effects, including wood grain, reflective sheen and crosshatching. It is usually done with a lay-in brush to insure consistency of grain over a wide area, but it can be done with any brush. The brush is dipped in paint, then as much excess paint as possible is removed by wringing out the brush on the edge of a bucket. The brush is then lightly dragged over the scenery so that each bristle or group of bristles produces a thin, distinct line.

Scumbling One commonly used texture technique is called *scumbling.* Scumbling is performed wet or dry for different purposes. Wet scumbling is used to create actual texture on old scenery that has been painted over many times and lost its textural weave.

This technique is also used on smooth materials like masonite to break up the surface. This is done by describing an "x" shape with the brush stroke. More random strokes can also be used, breaking up the smoothness of a surface even more. Wet scumbling can be used also to blend colors when no particular grain is indicated.

Dry scumbling uses the same brush stroke, but dry brushed on. This produces a random hatched look that suggests a rough, uneven surface.

Blending

One of the difficulties that beginning scene painters have in *blending* is that they end up mixing all the colors in the blend into one muddy color, when the intent is to blend different patches of color at their edges. It is important when blending to have a clean bucket of water nearby. Even if there is a separate brush for every color, each brush should be dipped in water after each application to help the blend colors retain their individuality.

When choosing colors for a blend, a combination of warm and cool colors should be considered. These will add a richness and depth to the scenery when other techniques are added on top of the blend. Wet blends are often used as undercoats or basecoats for other techniques. They provide a richness that cannot be achieved with simply a single-colored base coat. Usually the audience perceives this rich blend as a single color, and not as patches of three or four colors. It is called a wet blend because the areas of color are blended where they meet on the scenery while the paint is still wet. Each color is distinct, but it is hard to tell where one begins and the next one ends. Puddling must be avoided, although the paint must be wet enough to blend with.

When used as an undercoat for some material like wood or stone, two, three, or four colors should be chosen, and put on in relatively small patches in the same direction to suggest the grain of the material. Wet blends are used also when an area of the stage needs to be emphasized. The area to be stressed is based in a light color, which gradually blends into a darker outer area. This technique helps to draw the eye into the important acting areas.

Puddling is a technique that can only be achieved on the floor, and it produces a tie-dyed or watermark type of effect. In essence it is very wet blending. Puddles of paint are spilled onto the scenery (this spilling is controlled, however), and allowed to dry. This results in a rounded area of color, bordered by a thin line of the same color as the paint that seems darker than the

FIGURE 5–7. Wet blend

FIGURE 5–8. Puddling

general area of color (the watermark). Interesting effects can be achieved using single puddles, allowing several puddles to run into each other, or by allowing puddles to dry, and puddling over them again. This technique works especially well with glazes.

Dry blends are applied in very much the same way as wet blends are, but the edges of the colored areas do not fade into one another. Patches of color are painted on and allowed to dry before patches of the next color are put on. The patches are hard-edged, and thus appear to be rougher textured than a wet blend.

Spattering   *Spraying* and *spattering* are techniques for evenly applying a texture of little dots onto scenery. They are used primarily to soften the look of the painting, or to create a sense of depth or distance. The former is achieved simply because the dots of paint break up hard edges and lines without obliterating them. Also, gray or pastel spatters can tone undercolors that are too sharp. The latter is an optical illusion that suggests the effect caused by dead bugs on the wind shield of a car. If you focus on the bugs the scene outside becomes blurred, and vice versa. Spatter is indistinct enough to seem to be unfocussed nearby, making the scene appear as if it were farther away.

Uncontrolled spattering with a brush results in an uneven pattern of different sized dots and splatters. This technique is sometimes used to break up a surface roughly, such as a ground cloth in a forest scene. The brush is simply dipped into the paint and, without wringing it out first, the paint is flung off it, using the shoulder as a pivot point. (Do not let go of the brush!) Overhanded or underhanded techniques may be used. Each produces slightly different results, the latter providing a bit more control.

Brush spattering which produces a regulated distribution and size of paint dots is called a *controlled spatter*. The brush is held in one hand, and the ferrule is repeatedly struck against the heel of the other hand. It is not necessary to massacre your hand; a light touch will produce satisfactory results. The size of the dots is determined by how hard the brush is patted against the scene painter's hand and by how much paint is on the brush. These factors should be constantly adjusted as the paint on the brush is used up. Each time the brush is redipped a

FIGURE 5–9. Spatter

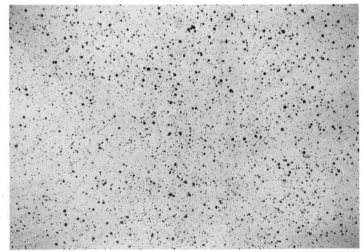

FIGURE 5–10. Holding a brush for a controlled spatter. It is hit against the heel of the other hand.

quick test spatter should be tried to double check that the new spatter is consistent with the old.

In general, wide brushes at least three-and-one-half inches wide should be used to spatter with. Thinner brushes tend to create lines of spatter that are difficult to camouflage. Usually spatter is used to create an even texture over a large area of scenery. Wide brushes not only avoid unsightly lines, but cover a larger area faster.

The more consistent and powerful the force pushing the paint is, the finer and more even the pattern of dots will be. This is why spraying produces a finer texture than spattering. No matter how controlled the spatter is, the pressure (inertia) that releases the paint onto the scenery is broken up by each beat of the brush. A spray is simply a spatter that is produced by a mechanism that uses air pressure to apply the paint with greater force.

The simplest sprayer is the plant mister. This is a plastic bottle with an aerosol pump. The pressure produced is uneven, but stronger than that produced when spattering. It is used for spraying small areas, because its range is limited to about a foot or two per spritz. As with all sprayers, the paint used should be as thin as possible, and must be strained before pouring it into the sprayer. The sprayer must also be cleaned immediately after each use to avoid clogging.

Pump sprayers are more commonly used. Because they provide relatively continuous air pressure the consistency of the spray they produce is pretty even. However, as the air pressure is used up the spray will become inconsistent and weak, and the nozzle may drip. Before each spray the sprayer should be tried out, to one side of the scenery. If it is producing the correct

FIGURE 5–11. Working with a pump sprayer

spray it should, without releasing the trigger, be moved onto the scenery. When the area of scenery to be sprayed is finished, or if it seems as if the sprayer is loosing pressure, the nozzle should be moved off of the area of the scenery, again without releasing the trigger, until the jet of paint is well off the work. Releasing the trigger changes the pressure to the nozzle, and if it is let go over the scenery the sprayer might produce unwanted drips. In between sprays the sprayer should be pumped up to assure a consistent spray overall. If a spray is to be repeated, it is not mandatory that the sprayer be cleaned out right away while the first spray is drying. It is helpful to stick the nozzle into a bucket of water so it will not clog. If the second spray is not to be applied for a long time the sprayer should be cleaned out, and the paint saved in a bucket.

Pneumatic sprayers provide a stronger and more consistent air pressure than pump sprayers, because as the pressure is used up it is automatically renewed by an air compressor. These sprayers are large scale air brushes and, as such, can produce a very fine, even spray. Often this type of spray is too fine to read on scenery, but provides a very soft area of color. It is sometimes used for stencilling, producing a soft, consistent area of color. The edges of the stencil design come out very distinctly because they are not broken up as much by the fine even application of spray.

Sometimes a part of the scenery needs to be sprayed but the surrounding areas do not. When these areas need to be clearly differentiated they can be masked off with masking tape and Kraft paper. When painting down, old masonite or other such sheets can be used.

Stippling

Stippling is a brush technique that uses the ends of the bristles. The brush is held perpendicularly to the surface of the scenery, and patted up and down with a quick, repeated motion. This produces a broken pattern of ferrule-shaped marks. The coarseness of the texture is controlled by how compactly the bristles are bunched, and by the thickness of the brush and amount of paint it is holding.

Feather Dusting

Feather dusting provides a marvelous texture for breaking up large areas. Larger dusters with long, stiff feathers work the best, although any type will work (even the silly looking ones with pink or yellow feathers that are sold in supermarkets). The feather duster is dipped into a palette tray of paint, then firmly stippled in another dry tray, to spread the feathers and remove excess paint. It is then stippled onto the scenery. Consistency of the texture is controlled by the volume of paint in the feather

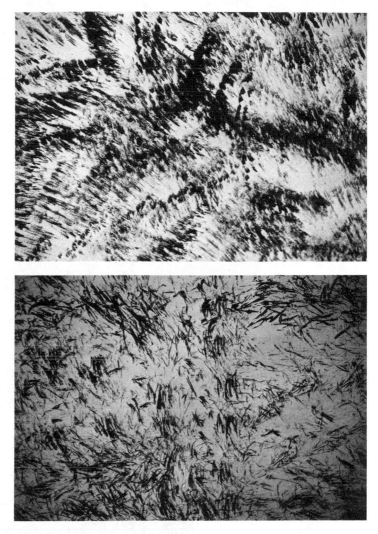

FIGURE 5–12. Stippling

FIGURE 5–13. Feather dusting

duster and the amount of pressure exerted. It is important to keep the right amount of paint in the tool. Too much paint will fill in the feathers and weigh them down so they will only produce unsightly blobs. As the paint is used up, the feather pattern will become smaller and fainter. A routine of painting and dipping should emerge that provides a consistent texture over the entire area being painted.

Sponging Natural sponges are the best for most scene painting because of their coarse-textured surface. They are used for many applications. Among the most common uses are foliage painting, stone texturing, and stencilling. Finer texture can be produced with synthetic kitchen sponges. When using these sponges the sharp corners should be rounded off by beveling them on a band saw, or just tearing them off. This allows the sponge to be used for its textural qualities without stamping a lot of rectangular sponge shapes onto the scenery. They can be used in their regular form, or cut into to stamp shapes and patterns.

The sponge is dipped in paint, then squeezed onto a clean palette tray to remove the excess paint. To produce a rough texture the sponge is stippled onto the scenery. A smoother texture can be produced by wiping the sponge instead of stippling it. By wiping in short, circular motions a good stucco effect can be produced. Wiping in parallel lines can give the appearance of reflections on a surface. When painting down the sponge can be bunched up on one side, and taped to a brush extender.

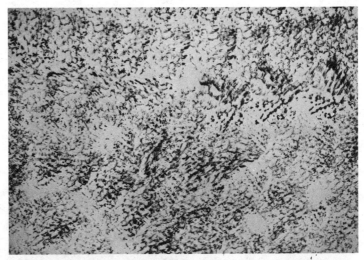

FIGURE 5–14. Stippling with a sponge

FIGURE 5–15. Wiping with a sponge

Rag Rolling   Another technique that yields a rough overall texture is called *rag rolling*. A fairly large rag of scrap muslin is dipped into a bucket of paint until it is completely saturated. It is then twisted until it becomes a long, club-like shape. It should be twisted quite tightly over the bucket to remove the excess paint. It should then be laid onto the scenery and rolled over it. The wrinkles and twists in the fabric produce the texture. This process is repeated when the fabric runs out of paint. Variations of texture can be achieved by using different fabrics. For example, burlap will produce an interesting texture.

Stamping   Stamping is used more often for repeat pattern techniques than as a texture technique, but textures of patterns can be created

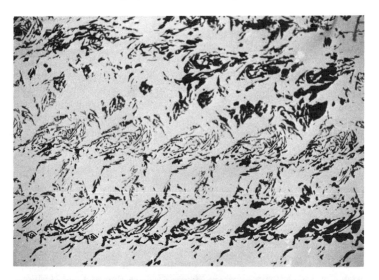

FIGURE 5–16. Rag rolling

FIGURE 5–17. A scene painter rolls a twisted rag over a flat.

FIGURE 5–18. Stamping

using stamps. It involves the use of foam rubber stamps that are cut out to represent different patterns and shapes. Explicit patterns such as leaves and flowers may be used, but very interesting textures can be produced using abstract stamps. Stamps can also be used in a logical pattern, but in this context they are stamped randomly all over the surface to be textured.

As with sponges, there are several ways in which a stamp may be used. The most obvious way is to stamp the shape onto the scenery with a stippling motion, creating a pattern of many identical forms. By holding the stamp at an angle to the scenery, half-shapes or simply outlines are created. A similar effect can be achieved by dipping only part of the stamp in paint. Different parts of the stamp, applied randomly, can effect any number of interesting patterns. Another approach is to drag the stamp across the surface of the scenery. A stamp that was originally cut to represent a pine tree can be used for combing or crosshatching by dragging one side over the scenery. The points, originally ends of branches, produce parallel lines.

Glazing

Glaze is put on scenery with brushes or sprayers. Glazing is used often for painted-on shadows, toning, sprayed fog, water, and for toning down colors that are too bright, among other uses. Because there is so much water in glaze, it tends to drip a lot when painting up. This can be avoided by using great care, or by painting down when using glaze. It works especially well in sprayers, because it is too thin to clog the mechanism.

Using a Roller

Paint rollers are rarely used for scene painting in the way they are used for house painting, except when they are used to paint a deck with a brush extender in the normal way. Several other

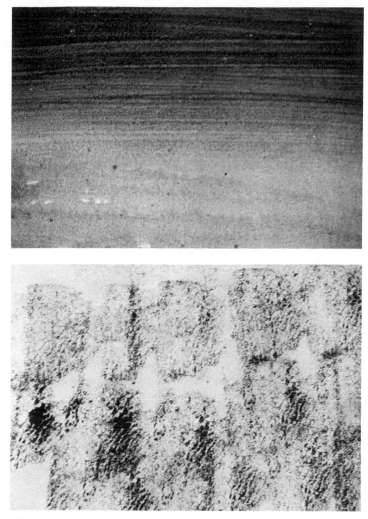

FIGURE 5–19. Glaze

FIGURE 5–20. Roller

effects can be achieved by using the roller imaginatively. Effects can also be varied by using different sizes of rollers and rolls with dissimilar naps.

A broken pattern can be produced by intermittently lifting the roller as it is being used. Rectangles and/or squares mix to form a broken pattern on the set. A variation of this technique is to push the roller against the direction in which it rolls, to produce thinner, fuzzy rectangular shapes or lines. Stippling with the roller will produce a similar effect.

By holding the roller at an angle the edge can be applied so it will paint thin lines or swirls. It can also be dragged across the scenery to create an effect resembling dry brushing.

Many varied patterns can also be created with rollers. Patterns can be cut out of thick-napped rolls with an X-acto® knife, or the roller can be bound simply with masking tape. Binding the roller with rags or rope will create several interesting patterns, as will wrapping it with textured fabric such as erosion cloth. Rollers with patterns cut out of them are also available commercially. Using these can be difficult since it is hard to keep the rows of the pattern lined up properly. The tool works much more satisfactorily when painting random textures.

6 Blending the techniques

PAINTING DIFFERENT MATERIALS

Once the basic texture techniques have been mastered they may be combined to simulate wood, marble, stone, drapery, foliage, or any other such material. The style of the painting is determined by the way the techniques are put together, as well as by the drawing style chosen for a set.

It is at this point that a "method" approach to scene painting breaks down. There is no method, for there are many approaches that will yield similar effects. The scene painter must choose an approach that will best result in the look that has been created by the designer. For example, there is an infinite number of ways to paint wood, and there are many different types of wood that could be painted. The basic approach to painting all of them is similar, but decisions on color, blending, dry brushing, and spattering can differ radically.

Although there is no hard-and-fast method, a methodical approach is helpful. Before beginning a painting project, the scene painter should develop a plan of action. Each step should be plotted out beforehand. This allows the scene painter to schedule the painting of each piece of scenery, to estimate the number of people needed to paint a specific project at given steps in its progress, and the amount of each color of paint needed to cover it. For example, a drop might need six gallons of paint for a complete base coat. If the coat is to consist of an equal blend of three colors, then only two gallons of each color are needed. Such a blend might take three painters one hour to finish, whereas a straight base coat might be finished by two scene painters in the same time.

Even when following a plan, the scene painter should stand back repeatedly to view the work in progress. Scene-painting techniques can be checked by standing about fifteen feet from the scenery and squinting slightly. When this is done, it becomes obvious whether or not an approach is working. If an approach is not working, the problem is often made apparent. If the techniques are too hard or distinct, a spray might be necessary. If the material does not look right, the colors might be off, the techniques inappropriate, or the style too tight or too broad. When this happens, steps in the plan are added or deleted as needed. When the painting is not working well and a better approach does not suggest itself, it is time to experiment on a test flat. Combinations of techniques can be tried quickly to find the best solution found.

It is important to remember how light and paint interact, and to give warm and cool stage lights something in the painting to react to, unless there is a specific reason for a purely monochromatic color scheme. The painted material must look natural under "sunlight" and "moonlight." Cool browns in wood, for example, or even blues, do not have to overwhelm the viewers' impression of a warm brown wood, but serve to keep the scenery from turning black when it is hit with blue light. Sometimes this is done in an underblend, with warm colors blended into cool. A warm spray over a cool painting can provide enough warm color to break up the lighting. Using warms for light and cools for shadows (the reverse is true when the assumed light source is supposed to be cool, such as moonlight), can help with the way the scenery takes light so it looks alright under unnatural light. Fitting cool colors into a warm palette, or vice versa, reads best when the colors are blended within the painting techniques. Merely adding a little spray afterwards can help, but may not work as effectively. Colors in an underblend may seem to be reading subtly, but they still make a strong impression that is difficult to cover up later. Using warms and cools both for colors in a blend, two colors of grain, marble veining, should be considered when working out a plan for painting each piece of scenery.

For every material that could be painted there are countless variations. There are hundreds of different woods, fabrics, plants, and so on. Oak wood requires a blend of light tans, with thin, fairly straight medium-brown graining technique. Mahogany requires darker, warm browns with free, wavy, dark-brown grain. Each variation on each material has attributes that are peculiar to it. It is essential, therefore, that a scene painter decide exactly what it is that is being painted before choosing colors and techniques to paint it with. There are many reference sources in which this information can be found. The first of these is the painter's elevations provided by the designer. Presumably he or she has done his or her homework and has indicated the desired material and how it should appear on the scenery.

When the elevations are incomplete, indistinct, or simply not present, there are still some very good sources of sample materials available. The best of these is an actual sample of the material itself. This does not mean the scene painter has to drive around until he or she comes upon an example of zebra wood to copy. Some of the companies that supply hard woods and veneers sell boxes of samples. These consist of either small blocks of each wood, or card-sized pieces of veneer, labeled with the name of the wood. These sets are inexpensive, and extremely useful. It is possible to compile a sample book of fabrics for painting draperies from the scrap bins in the costume shop, or the bargain counter in the fabric store.

When it is difficult to procure a collection of actual materials (a marble collection would be pretty unwieldy), books with color pictures are a good second best. Some volumes, published for architects and builders, will show sample swatches side by side for comparison. This is also true of suppliers' catalogs, especially those who do mail-order business. Volumes with color plates of historical architecture (Roman, Renaissance, and so on) provide good samples of various marbles, woods, stone, and so on. Field guides and other books about nature provide excellent examples of foliage.

When plotting the steps in painting a scene, the point at which the drawing will be done should be included in the plan. Usually the drawing is performed early in the process, after the base coat, since the drawing might require the grain to change in various areas. The drawing is done in charcoal first, then checked for accuracy and proportion. When it has been satisfactorily drawn and corrected it is carefully traced over with an ink marker. After inking is finished the whole piece is thoroughly flogged to remove any charcoal dust that might muddy the paint later on.

The color of the ink used should be dark enough to show through three or four layers of scene paint, but light enough to disappear after being painted over several times. These lines are simply guides for the scene painter, and should not be seen by the audience. Brown ink usually serves this purpose well, except when painted over with brown paint. Even when the lines are meant to show, the initial inking is intended only as a guide, and in such a case the lines should be redrawn over the other painting in the proper color and thickness. While painting, if the inked drawing begins to disappear before the painting is finished, it should be retraced with a marker.

Following are examples of painting various materials by blending the basic texture techniques. It should be remembered that these are examples, not prescriptions. They should serve as starting points on which variations can be tried. The examples illustrate the different kinds of choices that are made when painting scenery.

First, the type of material is chosen. Even when painting an abstract or cartooned version of a material, the more the scene painter knows about it before beginning, the more distinct the material will come out, and it will have more character. Based on this a step-by-step plan of action is decided upon for painting the basic material, which generally comprises the first stages of the painting. At the same time the final object or objects in the scene must be kept in mind so that the direction of the grain, sweeps of color, blending, and toning can be accounted for. Finally, the forms come out of the materials in the painting, with the emergence of perspective drawing, light and shade, and warm and cool colors.

Wood

When you look closely at virtually any natural object you will notice that it is made up of several colors or shades of a color. A piece of wood is unevenly colored with two, three, or four distinguishable colors. The grain of the wood is yet another color or two. Knot holes, worm holes, discoloration due to fading, add a still more uneven quality to it. This is why a wooden door, naturally finished, looks so rich next to a flat wall that has been painted a single color. The diversity in color and texture lends a rich dimensional quality to the wood. When you see a certain color of wood you are really seeing the sum of all the colors contained in it. The blends of color as well as the pattern and density of the grain and other irregularities are the qualities that make each type of wood visually unique. Visually understanding what a wood is made up of makes the choice of scene painting techniques to paint it more understandable.

The choice of the type of wood is up to the designer. This is based on a number of considerations. Period research, appropriateness to the script and the specific production, and the overall scheme of all the visual elements in the show are taken into account. Interiors of upper-class settings usually use fine-grained wood in deep, rich colors. Wood in rustic scenes tends to be coarse grained, with lots of knot holes. The type of wood to be painted suggests the scene painting techniques, and how broadly they should be used. Wood-grain painting oak and knotty pine use the same basic dry brush technique, but it is a good deal more delicate and controlled when painting oak.

The following example illustrates one approach to painting wood. The project is to paint a weather-worn pine-plank barn door. The planks will be broadly grained and distressed. The painting techniques will be broadly applied to suggest the textural quality of such wood.

This is a good point to consider the size of the theatre. In a small theatre the colors and techniques can be used relatively subtly. The audience is relatively close to the scenery and can discern differences in the texture, and in the hue and value of the colors. In a larger house the same techniques must be applied in much broader form. Subtle differences between color and brush techniques will not read beyond the third row. Such painting may look sloppy from the stage, but will be perfect as seen from the house.

The plan of attack for this project will consist of seven essential steps:

1. Base coat or wet blend
2. Drawing in charcoal
3. Inking in the drawing
4. Woodgraining and knot holes
5. Painting in cut lines
6. Highlighting and shading
7. Spattering

The first consideration is the base coat. This color should be chosen as close to the color of the finished door as possible. The color of the wood will be made up of several colors, so the base color should be close to the sum of all the colors in the wood. If a dry blend or scumble is intended, the base coat should be the neutral color of those that are to be painted. Depending on the size of the set piece, the base coat is painted on with a priming brush or a lay-in brush. Some care should be taken to avoid holidays since the white fabric will contrast noticeably, especially with darker paint colors. The base coat for the barn door is a neutral gray.

The next step is a blend. Three or four colors are chosen. Since the door is old and bleached by the sun, the wood has turned gray. The base color may be a neutral gray. A warm gray and cool gray should be used to give it depth and dimension, and to give different colored stage lights something to react to. Another way to vary the look of the wood is to vary the value of the colors. The warm gray might be lighter than the neutral, and the cool gray darker.

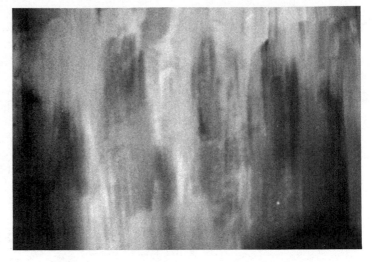

FIGURE 6-1. Wood: Wet blend

When using a wet blend, the base coat can be eliminated. Since the colors are blended when they are wet they must be put on at the same time overall, and thus a base coat is simply covered up by the blend. The wet blend thus becomes the base coat. The scene painter must watch for holidays, blending them into the painting when they occur. The barn door of our example is built out of vertical slats of wood, so the wet blend should suggest a vertical direction. Wood grain usually goes along the length of a board, so the vertical bias in the blend is called painting with the grain.

The next step is to draw the object made out of the wood, in this case the door. In this case the drawing is very simple, consisting of the vertical planks that make up the door and a cross plank and two horizontal planks that would be structural members if the door were real. Each plank is straight, even though the widths of the individual planks vary. With a charcoal stick, marks are made across the top of the scenery that represent the widths of the planks. This is done starting at one edge of the flat, used as a reference point from which all such marks will be made. An identical set of marks is made along the bottom with the exact same spacing between the marks.

An easy way to do this without having to measure each individual mark is to use a yardstick as an aid. When making the original set of marks on the top of the scenery, line up the yardstick with the starting edge of the flat, and hold it flat against its surface. When making the marks along the top of the flat, continue them onto the yardstick, creating identically spaced markings on the flat and the yardstick. To transfer the marks to the bottom of the flat, line up the yardstick along the bottom, making sure the same end is lined up with the same side edge

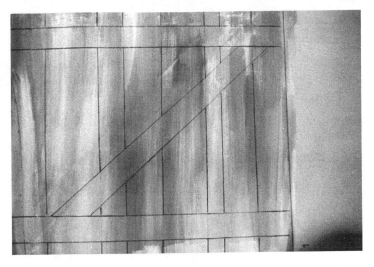

FIGURE 6–2. Wood:
Inked-in drawing

of the flat. Simply use the marks on the yardstick as a reference for the new set of marks. The charcoal easily wipes off the yardstick after the transfer is finished. In this way a run of marks can be quickly lined up a yard at a time, starting at one side of the flat, and starting the next segment of markings by lining up the end of the yardstick with the last mark from the previous yard. This method is a quick way to line up points for drawing any parallel lines.

When all the points have been found, the lines are drawn in between the top and bottom points. For short distances a yardstick or straightedge is used, drawing along its edge with a charcoal stick. Longer distances are snapped with a bow snap line. The diagonal plank is also drawn in, and all the drawing is checked for accuracy.

Next the drawing is inked in. The vertical lines are traced over the charcoal using a straightedge and ink marker. They should not continue through the horizontal or diagonal planks which are supposedly in front of them. When all of the lines have been inked in, the entire piece of scenery is flogged.

The lines that have been drawn in represent the spaces between the boards. These are called cut lines. Since the direction of the planks has now been defined by these lines, the wood may be grained. Wood graining should be painted on before the cut lines are painted so the scene painter will not stop the grained area short of the plank edges, trying to stay within the lines. If they are put in first there is a tendency to do this to avoid painting over the cut lines. This inevitably leads to a stripe on either side of each board that has not been grained. Graining the whole piece as if it were one huge plank avoids this problem. The audience will not notice whether or not the grain continues from board to board. From their distance they will only have an impression of the grain. They will perceive its direction and general thickness.

Dry brushing technique is used for wood graining. Broader graining is achieved by putting more paint and pressure on the brush, and more delicate graining by using a dryer brush and gentler touch. Most wood grain is darker than the undercolor, so a little black can be added to the darkest blend color to produce the grain color. This slightly darkens it without creating a stark contrast between the grain and the rest of the painting.

When a board goes in a different direction from the others, the grain must do the same. Thus, the graining on the diagonal plank must be diagonal, and horizontal on the horizontal planks. Before graining the direction of the blend may need some adjustment in these boards as well. Since on this project the area of these boards is fairly small, the blend direction should not significantly matter, and the plank direction will be defined by the direction of the graining, and by the drawing. This state of affairs is more likely to work with subtler blends. Coarser blends tend to assert themselves more through the covering techniques.

Wavy grain is painted on by holding the width of the brush perpendicular to the cut line. The brush is dragged in the general direction of the grain, then gradually to one side without tilting the brush. A semicircular motion creates a space in the graining in which to put knot holes. These are created by dipping the brush in the grain color and touching the corner of the brush to the scenery in a circular motion.

When the grain is to look very coarse, a second drybrushing of grain should be performed with a lighter color,

FIGURE 6–3. Wood: Graining

following the line of the grain already laid down. This will suggest that ridges of three-dimensional grain are sticking up and being hit by light from one side, and casting shadows from the other.

Now the cut lines are painted in with a yardstick and a liner. On our example a one-half-inch liner is used. The cut lines are painted in the darkest color, in this case an almost black gray. Cut lines are often, but not always, painted black. Very thin ones portray boards that are tightly spaced. Wider lines, as in this example, suggest that they are more spread out.

An imaginary light source is chosen. (This should be done in collaboration with the lighting designer so that painted shadows on the scenery will correspond with real shadows on stage.) In this example the light source is above the door and to the left. Two more colors are mixed: a light and a shadow color (the shadow may be paint or a glaze). Four edges show in the drawing of each plank: two sides, the top and the bottom. The two edges facing the light source—the top and left side—will be highlighted, and the other two will be shaded. Since the edges of the planks have not really been drawn in, the highlights and shadows should be very thin, used merely to suggest the three-dimensional quality of each plank.

All the shadows are painted in first with a dark cool gray glaze. When painting light and shadow, the colors are painted on one at a time, shadow first. Completely finishing each plank one at a time is both clumsy and time consuming. By painting all the shadows at once, the equipment does not need constant cleaning, and a pattern of dipping the brush and applying the shadow line can be established, assembly line fashion. First, the shadows on the right of each plank are painted in. The scene

FIGURE 6–4. Wood:
Painted cut-lines

painter's hands stay in the same basic position and movement patterns by moving the whole body along the scenery to paint each plank. When the side shadows are finished the bottom shadows are painted in similarly. Because the diagonal and horizontal planks stick forward from the rest of the door, wider shadows are painted on to illustrate their positions.

Shadows of straight objects must be even, unbroken lines, parallel to the edge of the object that is supposed to be casting the shadow. Care must be taken to keep the surface of the yardstick away from the scenery surface, and to distribute the paint consistently from the brush. If the brush will not make a long, unbroken line, it is possible that the paint is too thick. Watering it down can help the brush dispense it more fluidly. Another problem might be the quality of the brush. Poor quality brushes and brushes that have not been properly cared for do not hold as much paint or distribute it as consistently as good quality brushes in good condition.

Highlights are painted on similarly, but in thin broken lines. If you look at an object that is hit by direct light, you will notice the reflected glint of light on its edge is broken up. Using a small liner with a yardstick to paint randomly broken up lines will produce this effect. Common problems to be avoided include highlight lines that are too thick or broken up in a recognizable pattern. These read as clumsy paint lines, rather than glints of light.

The highlight for our barn door is a grayed cream color. Remember that paint with a lot of white mixed into it dries several shades lighter than it appears when it is wet. Loosely highlighting some of the knot holes makes them appear to be sticking out of the planks a bit. Shading them increases this illusion.

FIGURE 6–5. Wood: Shadows and highlights

FIGURE 6–6. Wood:
Finished project

Finally, the project is spattered. The first spatter is a broad controlled spatter in the shadow color. This will break up the smooth texture of the plank edges, and give a distressed look to the door. Next, glazes of a warm color (somewhere between the highlight and the warm blend color) and a cool color (the cool blend color) are applied in a fine controlled spatter. This adds some dimensionality and richness, and helps to give warm and cool lights more to react to.

Variations of this arrangement of basic techniques will produce any number of objects in different woods. To make wood painted in this manner appear to be stained or varnished an eighth step is added. A coat of clear, flat vinyl or latex is painted over the wood techniques. This restores the colors to the shades they appeared when they were wet, adding a rich quality to the "wood." A second coat of clear flat will make the wood seem even glossier. Usually clear gloss is not used, because it is so reflective that the details of the painting underneath disappear.

FIGURE 6–7a. Marble entablature.

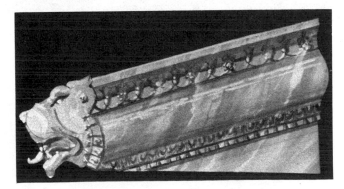

FIGURE 6–7b. Hardwood
entablature (top), and
gilt entablature.

FIGURE 6–8. Wood: Entablature project with light
and shadow. *Scene painter: Julie Roberts*

Marble The approach to painting marble is very similar to that of wood. The same principles apply, even though the two materials are very different. There are many types of marble, each with its peculiar color and veining characteristics. Sometimes more than one color of veining is distinguishable. Some marble veining is very distinct while other examples have fuzzy veins that look as though they are a little below the surface of the stone. This example deals with a simple marble block wall, painted in green and tan marble, with soft brown and green veins in it. The edges of the blocks are beveled. The plan of attack for this project includes seven steps:

1. Wet blend
2. Drawing in charcoal
3. Inking in the drawing
4. Veining
5. Spattering
6. Light and shading
7. Glazing

The soft-edged appearance of a wet blend lends itself to painting marble with its soft patches of coloration. Puddling also works well for some marble effects, but dry blends and scumbling are too harsh in texture. The colors chosen for this project are a green made by lightening chrome oxide, light raw sienna, and another light green with some blue in it. Since the stone blocks will be in horizontal rows, the blend is painted with a horizontal grain. This particular blend will use the neutral green as the dominant color, simply meaning that more of it is used than the other two colors in the blend. The ratio of the blend colors naturally affects the final color that is percieved by the audience. By making one color dominant it becomes essentially the color of the object which is toned by the other blend colors.

Drawing and inking is performed in the same way it was for the wood project. This time the stone blocks are uniform in size, two feet long by one foot tall. When marking points for drawing the cut lines, charcoal marks are placed on the yard stick every foot and corresponding marks are made on the scenery, along the top, bottom and both sides. The horizontal lines are snapped. Next, using a straightedge, the first vertical line is drawn through the first set of points, but only in the top, third, fifth, and all odd-numbered horizontal rows. The next vertical line is drawn through the next set of marks, but only in the even rows. The next is drawn through the odd, then the even, and so on, to produce staggered rows of marble blocks.

FIGURE 6–9. Marble: Wet blend
and inked-in drawing

FIGURE 6–10. Marble: Veining

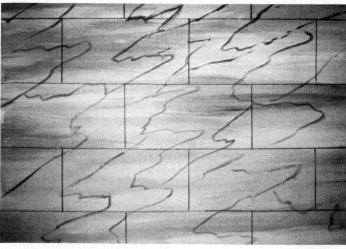

FIGURE 6–11. Marble:
Finished project

The two tools most often used for marble veining are the liner and the feather. Feathers were used in colonial America to simulate marble in civic buildings for which the colonies could not afford real marble. The technique they used was essentially the same as is used for modern scene painting. The wet blend must be completely dried so the paint in it is set up. The scenery is then wet again with a mister or a pump sprayer. The brush or feather is lightly held between the thumb and forefinger, and a random zigzag line is painted on, following a generally diagonal direction. This line should feather out a bit into the scenery. If it comes out with too hard an edge, it should be softened by spraying more water over it. The green veins are painted on this way, and then the scenery is allowed to dry again so the paint can set up. This step is then repeated for the brown veins, some of which follow the line of the green ones.

Painting marble can be very time consuming because the scenery must be continually wet again, then allowed to completely dry. If the paint is not given enough time to set up between steps, it merely blends into a muddy mess. Fans greatly reduce the drying time, but it is a good idea to have other projects to work on while waiting for the paint to dry.

A spatter or two will break up the flat surface of the scenery, but marble blocks are smooth surfaced, and should not be textured too much. A controlled spatter or a spray in the blue-green from the blend and, perhaps, a cream-colored glaze should break up the painting without making the surface seem too rough.

Because of the beveled edges, the light and shadow lines are thicker than they were on the wooden planks. A light source direction is chosen, and the two sides facing the source are highlighted, and the other two are shaded. The highlighted sides should be painted solidly with a light-colored glaze to show that the edges are at an angle, and the broken highlight put on over the glaze where the highlight would logically fall.

At this point the marble wall is substantially finished. If shiny marble is indicated a reflective shine can be painted on by dry brushing a diagonal glaze similar in color to the highlight, but with a little less white mixed into it so it will not contrast too extremely. This color should be tested over a sample of the marble colors to make sure it relates to them well. It is important that the dry brushing be perfectly straight, and that each brush stroke be parallel to the last one. Presumably the light will hit the surface of each block from the same direction, so the painted reflection must be consistent.

Clear flat may be used on marble in the exact same way it is used for glossing wood. This is often done on furniture and

FIGURE 6–12. Marble: Ionian column project. The marble technique is painted first, then the object is given form.

FIGURE 6–13. Marble: Entablature project. Scene painter: Steven Espach

other three-dimensional props, such as fountains, to make them seem more realistic.

Stone, tile, brick, and similar materials are painted with the same approach as wood and marble. The differences between them are mainly in the texture techniques chosen. Stones can be stippled with a natural sponge, as well as broadly spattered to portray their rough surface texture. Tile is very close to marble, but more opaque looking, and depends less on very wet painting. Slate or flagstone have distinct parallel grains to them accomplished by dry brushing clear flat over the painted slabs.

Drapery

Drapery requires a somewhat different approach, although the painting draws from the same pool of basic techniques. Special attention must be paid to the way real drapery hangs. Unlike wood and marble, the way fabric looks to us is dependent on the effect gravity has on it. It is easy to paint drapery badly, because the illusion of softly draped fabric is spoiled if it does not look like it is hanging naturally.

This example is a heavy Victorian-style drape of thick-napped maroon fabric with swags and tassels. The plan of attack will be:

1. Drawing and inking
2. Wet blending
3. Highlighting
4. Painting the trim

Perhaps the most important step when painting drapery is the drawing. Accurately portraying draped fabric can present some difficulties. For example, beginning painters tend to draw swags as simple arcs, when they are really comprised of several planes and bends that follow a roughly circular direction. The way a piece of fabric will hang is determined by gravity, the real (undraped) shape of the piece of fabric, and the stiffness of the cloth. The lines of pleated drapery tend to taper out at the bottom of the drape. The outside line of a swag appears as a number of straightish lines following a roughly curved pattern. Inside the swag are a number of folds and bends that actually do not resemble concentric areas.

The drapery is drawn in charcoal, and the drawing should be carefully checked. Mistakes are flogged out and redrawn. Only when the drawing is just right is it inked in.

Wet blending is used in a different way when painting drapery. The colors are blended to simulate the neutral color of the fabric, light, and shadow instead of a random blend of colors. This means that a light source direction must now be

FIGURE 6–14. Drapery:
Inked-in drawing

chosen. For this project the light is on the upper-right-hand side.

The colors are chosen with the light source in mind. A maroon color is mixed for the actual color of the drape. A blue-purple color and a medium yellow-cream are mixed for shadow and light. These colors will be blended logically according to the drawing and the light source. The scene painter has to be able to picture the drape in three dimensions, figuring out where the light would hit directly (from the right-hand side). The light paint will be used for these areas. The neutral (real color) will be used where indirect light would hit the material. The shadow color is painted in the folds of the fabric, where there would be no light. A liner or foliage brush is used for this blend, as most of the areas of color will be long and narrow. A fourth blend of color between the neutral and shadow colors will make the curves seem more gradual and rounded. The contrast between the neutral and shadow colors has to be fairly distinct for the shadows to read, so this in-between color softens the painting where sharp edges are not wanted.

The texture, or nap, of the fabric is suggested by the quality of the blend. Blends for thick-napped fabrics have a rougher quality to them. A less wet blend or even a dry blend, with the neutral color painted overall and the light and shadow painted over it, seems more textured because of the scratchy, distinct edges between the colors. The more gradual the wet blend, the smoother the fabric seems to be.

Once the blend has dried, highlight is added (a warm cream, lighter in value than the light blend color). This is also executed differently when painting fabric. Highlights may be thicker, unbroken lines, because, presumably the nap of the fabric is diffusing the light, causing a brighter area, but not a glint of light. Here again the thickness of the fabric's nap is implied by the pastiness of the highlight. Smooth, shiny fabrics like silk should have broken highlights painted on, in much the same way highlights are painted on wood or marble.

This simple combination of blends, applied logically according to an implied motivated light source, may be all that is needed to paint drapery. The blends can be softened still more with a light spatter or two in warm and cool colors.

Rope is simply painted, using three colors. The neutral (real) color is painted in a broken line, to suggest twists. The twists are then highlighted and shaded. The illusion is completed by painting the shadow of the rope on the underlying fabric, below and to the side away from the light source. This shadow will bend around the folds of the fabric, and its course should be plotted in charcoal to make sure it conforms with the shape of the drapery.

Fringe and tassels add a finishing touch. The basic fringe area is marked with charcoal. The neutral (real) color of the fringe is painted in vertical lines with a small liner. Even if the fringe is hanging off a swag the lines must be vertical, because real fringe always hangs straight down. Next the same area is painted with vertical lines in a shadow color. Spaces are left so the neutral lines show through. When that is finished the fringe is gone over with more vertical lines in a light color, again leaving spaces so the neutral and shadow lines show. Although the neutral, shadow, and light are painted on randomly, they suggest the uneven hang of many small strings. This row of fringe can be turned into a trim of tassels by painting a row of closely spaced round ball shapes directly over the fringe, using the same

FIGURE 6–15. Drapery:
Finished project

neutral color. Light and shadow colors are put in using a
scratchy dry-brush stroke according to the direction of the same
light source used for the rest of the drapery. The shadow color
is painted under each ball to suggest fringe bundled into tassels.

Some tassels are wrapped under the ball for a space before
the fringe emerges. When painting a more detailed tassel, more
drawing is needed. The wrapped part will resemble a cylinder
with the fringe below tapering out a bit. The same brush technique is used, but with the majority of the shadow color to one
side and most of the light color on the other. The strings that
wrap the tassel are painted on at a slight diagonal, then shaded
and highlighted to show that they follow a different direction
from the fringe. The shadow side should be shaded with some
neutral strings showing through, but no highlight on that side.
Such a tassel will cast a shadow on the drapery. As is true when
painting rope, the shadow should bend in the direction of the
folds of the drapery.

Skies There are several ways to paint a sky. This is done over a whole drop, on a drop as part of a scene, or on backing flats behind doors and windows. The simplest sky is white or light blue fabric. Canvas or muslin drops left their natural color, bleached, or dyed sky blue are commonly used. They depend on the lighting to provide visual interest and focus. The other extreme is a very detailed sky with clouds realistically painted on over sprays or blends that provide the illusion of distance.

Skies painted with blends of three or four colors are interesting because they change visually when the lighting changes. A very simple blend, painted with a priming brush or lay-in brush in horizontal strokes can be very effective. Warm and cool colors are blended so that when the color of the stage light changes on the scene, the composition of the sky also seems to change. The variation in color in the blend vaguely suggests clouds.

Using the same technique the eye can be drawn to a certain area of the sky by using more dark colors on the outside, and lighter colors where the scene painter wants to draw the audience's attention. In most shows the focus is downstage and roughly center, so dark toning in the blend should form a semicircular shape that deemphasizes the upper corners of the set. Differentiation of color in horizontal striations from a darker value to a lighter one will suggest distance. An occasional dark patch blended into the predominantly light area will provide interest by breaking up that area, and suggest an occasional cloud.

A similar effect can be obtained by using sprays instead of brushed-on blends. Horizontal striated sprays of three or four

FIGURE 6–16. Sky: Detailed clouds.
The Imaginary Invalid. Brandeis University.
Scene painter: Robert Moody; Designer:
Robert Little

FIGURE 6–17. Sky: Toned to draw the eye to the center. *Misalliance.* Brandeis University. *Scene painter: Robert Moody; Designer: Daniel Veaner*

FIGURE 6–18. Sky: Wavy, striated brush strokes. *The Victim.* George Street Playhouse. *Designer and Scene painter: Harry Feiner*

sky colors, warm and cool, will suggest soft, rolling clouds and provide a subtle background for a scene. The sky is first base coated white, blue, or light gray. Again, darker sprays in the upper corners will direct the focus down to the acting areas, and a loose progression from dark to light will suggest distance. This is a quick method of painting an effective sky.

One interesting brush technique for painting skies blends colors in striations of wavy lines. These can be blended wet or dry. The waves read as a textural quality that may suggest clouds, distance, or simple visual interest. Such a sky changes noticeably with lighting changes. Variations can be achieved by using greater or lesser contrast between the colors of the blend.

Skies can also be painted explicitly with accurately drawn clouds. The sky area is base coated, and can be sprayed or blended to give a sense of distance. The cloud shapes are drawn

PLATE 1. This detail from *The Plow and the Stars* shows a variety of texturing materials. The posters are canvas appliqué, the wooden door is textured with scenic dope and with appliquéd foam cross-beams, the brick arch is vermiculite mixed with glue, the beveled stones are homosote cut-outs, and the rough stones are foam. *Scene painter: Robert Moody; Designer: Harry Feiner*

PLATE 2. Texture is provided on this set piece for *The Plow and the Stars* by using different fabrics, including canvas, scrim, and bobbinet, and by carved foam ornaments.
Scene painter: Robert Moody;
Designer: Harry Feiner

PLATE 3. (*above*) Set piece for *The Mikado*, painted as a translucency. The fan is starched and painted with very thin paint on the front. There is no back paint, which allows the skeletal bracing of the unit to show through when backlit.
Scene painter: Daniel Veaner

PLATE 4. (*left*) Old-fashioned-style wing-and-border set for *Little Mary Sunshine* with cut foliage borders. Foreground foliage is stamped on with a cartooned leaf shape. Background foliage is also stamped. The drop is heavily distressed before painting so it will look like an old stock melodrama drop.
Scene painter: Daniel Veaner

PLATE 5. (*below left*) This drop from *Pippin* is horizontally hatched with priming brushes. The texture in the hatching comes from a rough shop floor. The figures are cartooned over the hatching, and the drop is finished with a toning spray. Erosion-cloth banners are framed with cut-out muslin appliqué. The muslin is stretched and painted before cutting out to avoid shrinkage.
Scene painter: Daniel Veaner

PLATE 6. Warm and cool colors help the perspective drawing in this painter's elevation to create a sense of depth. Color samples are provided for the scene painters to match.
Designer: Daniel Veaner

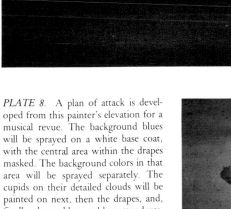

PLATE 7. The drop is painted using a lot of sprays and glazes. The window is painted as a translucency so it may be lit from behind.
Scene painter: Robert Moody

PLATE 8. A plan of attack is developed from this painter's elevation for a musical revue. The background blues will be sprayed on a white base coat, with the central area within the drapes masked. The background colors in that area will be sprayed separately. The cupids on their detailed clouds will be painted on next, then the drapes, and, finally, the goddess and her attendants. A final spray will soften the picture.
Designer: Daniel Veaner

PLATE 9. Detail of drop for *Uncle Vanya*. Background is sprayed with a pump sprayer and hatched in with a brush. Trees and foliage are put on with brush techniques. Birch bark is painted with simple horizontal curves. *Scene painter: Robert Moody; Designer: Melinda Leeson*

PLATE 10. All the clapboard in this set for *Picnic* is painted on flats. Hard covered flats are covered with scenic dope, which is textured before painting. *Designer and scene painter: Harry Feiner*

on realistically. Clouds are then painted a neutral color, and then shaded and highlighted. These colors are painted on using a motivated light source from one side.

Translucencies Translucencies can be very useful when creating a sunset on a painted sky. The drop should be seamless, or at least no seams should run through the area of the translucency. If this technique is used on framed scenery there must be no toggles cutting through the translucent area. This technique is used on muslin only, because it is thinner than canvas, and lets light through more efficiently.

The muslin is sized or starched first on the back. When it has dried, the fabric is turned over and sized on the front. Because it will be painted on the back and the front, both sides need to be sealed. This means that holidays in the prime coat have to be especially avoided, because they might let splotches of color seep through from one side of the drop to the other.

Clouds are drawn onto the fabric. The front of the fabric will have the day sky painted onto it, so the clouds should be distributed all over. When the drawing has been completed and checked, it is inked in.

The muslin is turned over again, and those clouds that will be used for the translucency are traced on the back with an ink marker. These are clouds that are low on the horizon that are the last to be seen before dark. The inking from the front will show through, and these clouds should be exactly traced from the front drawing. The rest of the back of the fabric is painted with opaque black paint, silhouetting the drawn-in clouds. These are then painted with red, lavender, and amber aniline dyes. Thin casein can be used instead of aniline dye, but the colors will not be as brilliant.

The scenery is turned over one more time, and the sky and clouds are painted on the front with very thin paints and glazes.

To make it work the sky is lit from the front in daylight colors. As the scene progresses the lights fade slowly. At the same time lights hung behind the sky are faded up, causing the brilliant dye colors to show through the chosen clouds, while the light is masked out by the opaque paint around them.

With imagination, this effect can be put to many uses. Translucencies can be used to make a stained-glass window painted on a church scene stand out brilliantly from the walls of the church. Objects, messages, and symbols can be made to appear out of nowhere on walls, or skywriting in the sky. The possibilities are endless.

Water

Painted water in lakes, rivers, and so on is achieved in much the same way skies are. Striations of wavy lines of glaze, applied with liners, produce a body of water. Calm water is painted with fairly straight lines, choppy water with wavy lines, and very rough water may have white caps painted in.

Reflections of objects define painted bodies of water. They must be blended into the water technique, using colors resembling the objects that are reflected, blended with some water colors. In general, reflections are painted below the object. It should be kept in mind that an object such as a boat will cast a shadow onto the water in addition to its reflection. Because there is so much reflected light in daylight the shadow will be only near the water line, making that part of the reflection seem darker.

Foliage

Virtually all of the texture techniques are used to paint foliage. Leaves form a textured pattern made up of many small leaf patterns repeated over a large area of scenery. There are several approaches to suggesting the wide variety of leaves that exist in nature.

When painting a tree or bush the general shape is sketched in first. The trunk, branches, and twigs are located, and leafy areas are outlined around them in charcoal. (These should not be inked in, because the leaves may or may not fill the whole area. After they are painted in, the charcoal is flogged away.) The branches and trunk are painted first, so they will show through the gaps in the leaves. Then the leaves are painted on, confined within the areas defined for them.

Most foliage is green. Green paint can be lightened with white to produce a chalky looking pastel, or with light yellow

FIGURE 6–19. Water: The water is defined by the reflections. *Scene painters: Lori Willis; Linda Cappeletti*

which produces a more natural color. Browns, oranges, yellows, and blues can be blended in with the greens for modelling, texture, light and shading, and to suggest the inconsistencies found in nature.

Trunks and leafy areas should be considered as three-dimensional objects. This means a light source direction is chosen, and all the foliage is painted accordingly. At least three colors, representing the neutral, light, and shadow should be used for the wooden parts, and three or more other colors used to paint the foliage. This should not imply that, in a leafy clump, one side is painted with light leaves only and the other painted exclusively with dark leaves. The colors should be intermixed, with the majority of dark leaves on the shadow side, and so on. Although the leaves form in clumps to form a collective shape, they are also individual objects. Sometimes one, or a small clump, will stick out of a shaded area to catch some light, and other times leaves in a lighted area will be shaded, because they are back inside the clump a bit.

Although the leaves are usually indicated in the drawing by a general area, the wooden parts of the tree are explicitly drawn on. In general a tree trunk is thicker at the ground, and gradually tapers as it goes up. Branches are thickest where they join the trunk, or sprout off another branch. The joints of branches are ususally marked by a small bulge and a distinct bend.

The trunk and branches are based in a brown, gray, or other appropriate color. Light and shadow colors are chosen, and painted on to suggest their roughly cylindrical form. Texture techniques for bark may include short, overlapping brush strokes, sponging, or stamping. Sponging on moss can be very effective. When applying the texture, the basic form must be kept in mind and maintained by using light and shadow colors in the texture technique. Sometimes a broken highlight increases the illusion of form.

The placement of foliage in a scene will help to determine the texture technique used to paint it. Scenes can be divided into a foreground, middleground, and background. The size of leaves is larger in the foreground, and smaller as they go back in perspective. In such a scene the background is always painted first. It should be painted over the drawing for the middle- and foreground, so that it will show through gaps in the nearer foliage. The scene painter works forward from the background, painting the nearer objects over those farther away.

Background foliage is usually pretty small in scale, and reads as a texture, defined only by its general form as delineated by the basic shapes and light and shadow. Stippling areas with a sponge, stippling with a brush, and rubber stamping are some ways to quickly achieve background foliage. Whole trees can be stamped onto a scene, thus foliating an entire forest in minutes!

Middle- and foreground foliage can be painted in any number of ways. The most basic technique is executed with a foliage brush. The side and flat of the brush are pressed onto the scenery, creating a leaf shape. With practice, a typical leaf, starting with a point and widening into curved sides that end with an arc or another point, can be painted by twisting the brush slightly as it is pressed to and released from the scenery. Other kinds of leaves can be painted by patting the side or the flat of the brush onto the scenery.

Foliage thus painted can be given added dimension by painting leaves in light and shadow colors. Cartooning around the edges, or painting in a central vein distinguishes each leaf. Spattering suggests worm holes, tears and other irregularities.

Very large leaves are painted like any object would be. They are drawn out first, then based, shaded, and highlighted. Veins and other features are painted on with a liner.

Grassy leaves are painted with the end of the brush, holding the width of the ferrule on end so the thin expanse of the bristles creates the blade of grass. Starting thick at the bottom pressure is lessened on the brush as it is moved up, so the leaf will taper, finally ending in a point.

Evergreen leaves and needles are also painted with a foliage brush, using a dry brush technique. It is important to maintain the shape of the needle clumps by changing the axis of the brush stroke. Some evergreen needles are short, others, such as pine, are long and curved. The particular type of tree being painted should be researched, and the correct pattern of needles emulated.

Feather dusting produces pretty good fern leaves. The duster has to be controlled, or may even have to be trimmed to get all the leaves to face in the right directions.

Foam rubber stamps can produce any variety of foliage, because the stamps are custom designed and built in the paint shop for whatever type of leaf is needed. A time-saving device is to design a stamp with a clump of about five leaves on it. The shape of the leaf clumps can be varied by holding the stamp in different directions, or by stamping it at an angle some of the time so that only one or a couple of leaves are stamped.

Once foliage has been painted on by whatever method, it should be textured further, usually with a series of spatters. Broad spatters over bunches of leaves increase the variety, depth of field, and richness of color of the painted foliage.

FIGURE 6–20. Foliage: Texture and foliage techniques mixed to paint foliage.

FIGURE 6–21. Foliage: Brush techniques used to paint a scene.
Scene painter: Lee Ann Chamberlain

FIGURE 6–22. Foliage: Brush techniques in the foreground, sponge stippling in the background.
Scene painter: Karen Andersen

FIGURE 6–23. Foliage: Brush
techniques using shadow and light
colors. *Misalliance*. Brandeis University.
Scene painter: Robert Moody;
Designer: Daniel Veaner

FIGURE 6–24. Foliage: Plastic foliage
is painted to match painted
foliage underneath to provide a
sense of depth. *Misalliance*.
Brandeis University. *Scene painter:*
Robert Moody; Designer: Daniel Veaner

126

PAINTING A SCENE

Blending the texture techniques to create a type of material is all that is needed for some sets. Often three-dimensional scenery has sufficient form to portray what is needed visually, and thus only needs to be painted to simulate the material it is supposed to be made of. Others require a more complicated scene to be painted on a single surface.

When painting a scene on a drop, many of the methods already described are put together, along with drawing, in perspective. After the drop has been prepared and the drawing completed and inked in, the painting starts with the most distant part and advances to the foreground. A plan of attack is developed for the whole scene.

Following are some examples of painting scenes step by step:

London street drop. This project is executed by three scene painters over a two-day period on the shop floor on a muslin drop twenty feet by forty-two feet. The first morning is spent stretching the drop out on the floor. The two assistants work on this project. The drop is starched and gridded, and all three scene painters work on the drawing. As the drawing is finished, the charge man begins to mix colors. Starting with the background, which is at the top of the picture, the drop is painted toward the foreground. The painters frequently change places so their individual styles will be mixed up in the painting. By the end of the first day the drawing and inking has been finished, and some sprays have been put on. Much of the second day is spent painting details.

FIGURE 6–25. Painter's elevation for London street drop

FIGURE 6–26. Scene painters draw in the design on a gridded drop, using drawing sticks and extended straightedges.

FIGURE 6–27. The corrected drawing is inked in. After this step, lay-in brushes on brush extenders are used to put in areas of color.

FIGURE 6–28. Details are cartooned in with a liner.

FIGURE 6–29. A scene painter puts in
detail painting, carefully referring to the
painter's elevation.

FIGURE 6–30. The finished drop. *Spring Dance
Concert*. Rockford College. *Scene painters:
Daniel Veaner, Steven Espach, Anne Hubbard*

Cathedral drop. This project is executed on a twenty-two foot by forty-two foot muslin drop on the shop floor. It is painted in just over a day by a charge man and six assistants. It will be part of a set for a modern dance entitled *Cathedral*. In the afternoon of the first day, a few assistants staple down the drop, first preparing the floor and laying down Kraft paper. The drop is starched and gridded so painting may begin without delay the next morning.

FIGURE 6–31. The painter's elevation is drawn to 1/2-inch scale. Color samples are indicated along one side. The elevation has been covered with acetate and gridded beforehand so the crew will not have to wait to paint.

FIGURE 6–32. Using the gridded elevation as a guide the design is drawn onto the drop. Several scene painters work at once, using drawing sticks and straightedges with extended handles. A gridded set of photocopies or blue-line prints of the elevation help this step to go faster, because working from individual copies the scene painters do not have to run back and forth to share the original.

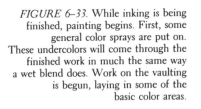

FIGURE 6–33. While inking is being finished, painting begins. First, some general color sprays are put on. These undercolors will come through the finished work in much the same way a wet blend does. Work on the vaulting is begun, laying in some of the basic color areas.

FIGURE 6–34. Detail drawing is done with liners and a foam rubber paint applicator. The applicator has been cut so its edge resembles teeth to facilitate hatching in the drawing.

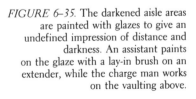

FIGURE 6–35. The darkened aisle areas are painted with glazes to give an undefined impression of distance and darkness. An assistant paints on the glaze with a lay-in brush on an extender, while the charge man works on the vaulting above.

FIGURE 6–36. The drawing is finished.
Hatching is put into the nave arcade to suggest
the space in the aisles.

FIGURE 6–37. Sprays of color radiate from the window to suggest light rays. The light source for this drop is the window, and light and shadow are painted on accordingly. The final step is to paint areas of payne's gray glaze around the corners, which help bring the focus towards center, and create the oval-shaped composition indicated on the elevation by the designer.

FIGURE 6–38. The finished drop is hung on a batten on stage. *Spring Dance Concert.* Rockford College. *Scene painter: Robert Moody; Designer: Daniel Veaner*

Landscape demonstration. This drop is a paint demonstration painted in an afternoon on the floor on a drop about twelve feet by twenty-five feet.

FIGURE 6–39. The drop has been stapled down and starched. The drawing is put on. Because this demonstration is limited in time, the scenic artist has sketched his design onto the muslin quickly from his head. Attention is given to details to ease the painting process later. Careful drawing saves time later in the painting, because the composition will be set.

FIGURE 6–40. Warm and cool color sprays define space, provide undercolor, and give a sense of depth to the drawing.

FIGURE 6–41. Texture techniques begin to define
individual objects. The textures add to the
richness of the composition. The imaginary light
source is to the left.

FIGURE 6–42. The drop is finished with more
precise brush techniques. *Scene painter and Designer:
Robert Moody*

7 Repeat patterns and graphics

Many times a scene design will call for a repeat pattern of some kind. It might be an ornamental decoration on a trim, a pattern to suggest texture, or a wallpaper pattern. Some patterns require high definition while others are merely suggestive. Patterns can be highly ordered as in a wallpaper pattern, or random, like leaves on a tree. A repeat pattern on scenery should be a suggestion to the audience. It should be perceived and accepted by them without beckoning their conscious attention. Wallpaper should be suggested softly. The audience should think they are seeing wallpaper so they can accept it and forget it. It should be part of the environment surrounding, but not dominating, the drama.

Pattern equipment is used for both speed and accuracy in scene painting. Free-hand pattern painting would take an age, and the result would not be uniform enough to portray a pattern believably. Patterns can enhance a set, giving it a larger textural quality as well as suggesting a particular object, shape or design. When working out a pattern, there is a danger that the scene painter might concentrate only on the individual shape to be repeated. That shape, in different configurations, can create widely varying looks. Overlapping, using several colors, and different techniques for applying paint all determine the finished result.

Usually the scenic designer will provide a design of the pattern and/or a clearly scaled painter's elevation. The elevation will indicate how the pattern is to be applied, spaced, and lined up, how distinct it should be, what other techniques should be used, colors, toning and so on. The rendering will show the sort of atmosphere the designer is trying to portray, which is also helpful when deciding on the method of application for the pattern.

Pattern-making equipment is manufactured in the paint shop. The three types of equipment that are commonly used are *stencils, pounces,* and *foam rubber stamps.* Stencils are the most common and the easiest to use, but stamps are the most fun.

Stencilling

Stencils range from about one square foot to a couple of feet. If they are constructed too large they are unwieldy, and must be reinforced with wires. Most stencils have only one example of the pattern cut out of them unless the pattern is small enough to fit a group on a single stencil.

The first step is to draw the pattern design. The size of a single pattern is determined and a box is drawn on a sheet of stencil paper to that size. The pattern will be drawn inside the confines of this box. A pattern that will be self-contained should be drawn well within the box so that when it is repeated it will not touch itself. An entwining pattern must be matched at the points where it will meet itself.

To match an entwining pattern the design is sketched in lightly with a pencil. Some patterns repeat evenly above, below, and next to each other. Others are staggered. Matching an entwining pattern when it is not to be staggered is really quite simple. Any line that will continue from one form to the one next to it must go off the pattern on the right at the same height it goes off on the left. When the pattern is repeated next to itself the two lines will seem continuous. Often, especially in the case of wallpaper patterns, the patterns will be staggered so that a form will begin half way from the bottom of the form next to it. In this case the lines on the right and left sides will go off the stencil at different heights. For example, if the line on the right goes off two inches below the top of the stencil, the line on the left must go off two inches below the center of the stencil. When staggered the lines will meet. Patterns that match up in this way tend to form larger diagonal patterns that may not be wanted. Care should be taken to break up the larger pattern that is formed by joining the individual designs elsewhere on the sides and top to bottom, unless there is a particular dramatic purpose for the larger diagonal.

Once the pattern has been drawn on the stencil paper so that it works well, the lines should be thickened so they can be cut out. Lines thinner than one-half inch will be difficult to paint through the stencil, and will probably be too small to show up effectively on most scenery. Long lines and large shapes are tabbed to hold the stencil together when it is used. A *tab* is a break in the cut-out line. The tabbing should be figured out in pencil before beginning to cut out the pattern. At the distance the pattern will be seen by the audience, the tabs are

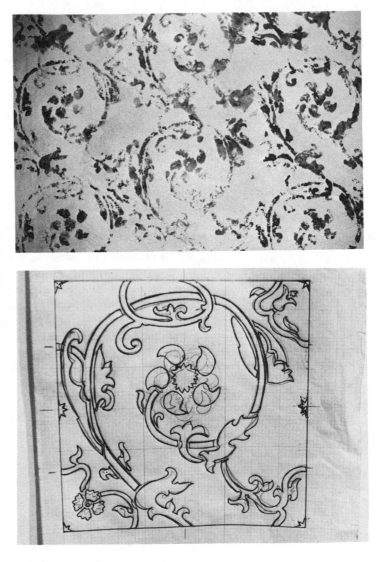

FIGURE 7–1. Stencil:Matching a
pattern, using six register
marks to stagger vertical rows

FIGURE 7–2. Stencil: Design
for a wallpaper pattern

unlikely to show, so stencils should be tabbed generously. It is
better to have too many tabs than too few; if the stencil falls
apart in use it is worthless. Lines broken by tabs seem continuous because the eye perceives them that way in spite of the
breaks. Often the tabs can be incorporated into the design.
When all the tabs have been drawn in and the pattern lines
look natural, they can be cut out with an X-acto®knife. When
cutting a symmetrical stencil, half the stencil is drawn and cut
out. The stencil is laid over another piece of stencil paper and
spray painted. The original half-stencil is then turned over and
lined up exactly at the center line and spray painted again. This
provides a whole pattern, which may be cut out now.

Now *register marks* must be added. These marks are used to line up the pattern so that it repeats itself with equal spacing each time. A simple, unstaggered pattern needs one register mark in each corner of the original square that was drawn. These marks can be small squares, diamonds, and the like, which will barely show up on the finished work, or larger, integral or independent parts of the pattern. Staggered patterns require three register marks on each side. The third mark is placed halfway between the top and bottom marks. To stagger the pattern the center mark is matched with the top and bottom marks of the two patterns stencilled next to it.

A 1 by 1 frame is constructed for the stencil. It should be bigger than the surrounding square boundary by at least three inches on each side to allow room for a sponge to get in. The frame is centered on top of the stencil, and the stencil paper is cut to the frame size. It is then glued and stapled to the frame.

Finally, the stencil should be shellacked on both sides. This lends strength to the stencil and helps to waterproof it. An easier but more expensive way to seal the stencil is to apply three coats of spray paint on each side. Six coats is a lot of spray paint, and not very good for the lungs, so this operation should be carried out in a well-ventilated work space.

Several spare stencils should be built for each pattern that is used. The spares are rotated during stencilling so that no individual one gets too soggy. There should be at least two copies

FIGURE 7–3. Stencil: Finished stencil

FIGURE 7–4. Stencil: Design for a border pattern

FIGURE 7–5. Stencil: Finished border stencil

per scene painter. The original is laid over a new piece of stencil paper. The outside of the frame is traced with a pencil. Then spray paint is sprayed through the stencil, creating a pattern on the new sheet. This is simply cut out, framed, and shellacked. Any number of identical patterns can be constructed in this way.

Wallpaper. Before discussing wallpaper stencilling, it should be noted that sometimes real wallpaper is hung on a set. Real wallpaper has the advantage that a complex multicolor pattern is already stencilled on it and need only be hung up. However, it also presents problems because it is designed for real homes, not stage scenery. It is often difficult to find the right-sized pattern in the desired design at an affordable price. The finish is often too smooth and reflective, and wallpaper patterns tend to be small by stage standards. Wallpaper must be applied with wheat paste or wallpaper paste to hard-covered flats. Wallpaper pasted on soft-covered flats wrinkles and tears easily (a nice effect when portraying an old, distressed interior). Usually wallpaper will be enhanced with scene paint, including additions to the pattern, and spatter or sprays to unify it with the rest of the set. The main disadvantage of using real wallpaper is that it forces the designer and scene painters to relinquish most of their control over what can be a major visual element in the setting.

Creating wallpaper with stencils allows a lot more artistic control. The shape of the design, the frequency of the repetition, the texture of the wall surface, the color and finish of the pattern, are determined by the designer and communicated to the scene painter via the painter's elevations and pattern detail.

Figuring out the overall pattern falls within the designer's province, but the scene painter is also involved. There are many possible varieties. The pattern may be evenly aligned or staggered. A uniformly aligned pattern will create a larger pattern on the wall, much like the individual squares on a checkerboard do. Greater variety can be achieved by making every other pattern a different color, or by skipping every other one. Staggering the pattern will usually break up the area in a more interesting format, making each group of four patterns suggest a diamond shape. Joining such a staggered pattern with connecting lines from the sides will create a diagonal emphasis. Joining patterns top to bottom creates a vertical design. Patterns can be mixed with some other repeated design element, such as stripes. A row of patterns vertically stencilled between stripes will create an interesting design. Another variation is to use double stripes, then a row of patterns. Still another is to paint a stripe, a row of pat-

FIGURE 7–6. Stencil: The wallpaper and border
stencils applied to a set. *Hay Fever.*
Brandeis University. *Designer and Scene painter:*
Daniel Veaner

terns, a stripe, a blank space, and so on, repeating this sequence.
The possibilities are unlimited.

Sometimes the designer will choose to use more than one
pattern for wallpaper. Many Victorian wallpaper designs, for example, use a top and/or bottom border with the main stencil
pattern in between. Occasionally, there will be still another pattern between the molding on a double cornice.

The scenery needs some preparation before stencilling begins. Of course it must be base coated and/or blended. Sometimes a blend will emphasize a particular part of the set. After
stencilling over it, the blend is less obvious, but still the eye is
drawn to the desired spot. The distance between the register
marks, right to left, is measured. That measurement is transferred to the set, starting in one corner, and continuing all the
way across. If, for example, the measurement is eighteen inches,
a mark will be made every eighteen inches across the top of the
set. Identical marks are made at the bottom of the set. If, at the
end of a flat there are only six inches left, then the first mea-

surement on the next flat will be only twelve inches. (The flats must be painted in order, as they will be assembled on stage.) When the two flats are joined to make a corner it will look like the wallpaper was hung around the corner, because the pattern will be continuous. Charcoal lines are snapped with a bow snap line from the top set of marks to the bottom set. These lines should be double checked to make sure that they are, indeed, vertical. They will be the guide lines along which the register marks on the stencil will be aligned.

The method of application of paint through the stencil will have an important impact on how the pattern turns out. Sponging the pattern will provide an indistinct, fuzzy pattern that is often desirable, because it prevents the wallpaper from "popping out" of the set. The sponge is dipped into the paint, dabbed on a palette tray to get rid of excess paint, and stippled through the stencil. A firm, even-handed stipple should be used. The whole pattern should not be filled in. The point of using the sponge in the first place is that it will provide a soft texture that will simply suggest the pattern. A grain can be suggested by dragging the sponge over the stencil, or by using a quick turning motion of the wrist. Care must always be taken not to put too much paint in the sponge, or to apply too much pressure, for the paint will be wrung out and will drip down the back of the stencil, ruining the scenery.

Stippling or painting the stencil with a brush provides a somewhat more distinct pattern. A two-inch foliage brush works well. When stippling with a brush, the direction of the ferrule should be constantly changed to avoid a series of ferrule-sized lines that may cause an unwanted pattern. A thick, round-ferruled stencilling brush is made for stencilling, and will not leave such a pattern.

To get a very distinct pattern, a pneumatic paint sprayer may be used. This is a large version of an air brush. Quick squeezes of the trigger allow the work to be seen in progress, and reduces the danger of excess paint dripping down the back of the stencil. It may be necessary to mask around the stencil frame with more stencil paper so the spray will not go over it, causing the hard lines of the frame to show up.

When painting, the stencil is held against the scenery with one hand and the paint applied with the other. Care must be taken regularly that the register marks are all on the guide lines. If they are not, it usually means that the stencil is crooked. The registers should be painted through each time the stencil is, so they can be matched for repeating the pattern in the correct positions.

When stencilling a multicolored pattern it is not necessary

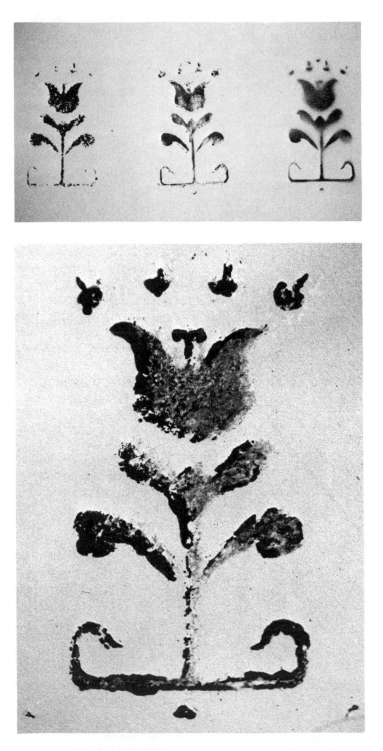

FIGURE 7–7. Stencil: Three methods of application: (right to left) sponged, brushed, and sprayed

FIGURE 7–8. Stencil: Flocked wallpaper technique, created by painting the stencil again, slightly misaligned

to create two or more partial-pattern stencils. The full shape is cut out, then areas not to be included in the first color area are closed with masking tape. When the first color has been stencilled over the entire set, the open areas on the stencil are masked and the tape is removed from the area of the second color. This process is repeated for each color used.

Flocked patterns can be simulated using one stencil with two colors. The wallpaper is sponge-stippled on the scenery as it would normally be done for a one-color, one-pattern design. When this has dried, the stencil is slightly misaligned over each painted pattern, and lightly stippled again in another color. The misalignment of the stencil must be consistent from pattern to pattern. If the stencil is slightly to the right on one pattern, it must be slightly to the right of all the patterns in the same set. When seen from a distance the pattern will look slightly raised and fuzzy.

Occasionally a very complicated pattern will require two or more stencils to be overlayed. It is very important that the register marks be identical on each so that the pattern will fit together properly in its finished form. Some intricate and striking patterns can be made this way.

Bricks. Painting bricks with a stencil can provide a very realistic effect when skillfully used with other techniques. Some sets call for a cartooned look, and on these the mortar lines are stencilled onto a brick-colored base coat. A more realistic result is obtained by stencilling the bricks over a mortar-colored base coat. The color of the mortar is usually some variation on gray. Spattering with darker and lighter grays breaks up the base coat. Guide lines are snapped in charcoal for the register marks on the stencil, and the bricks are then sponged on through the stencil, covering most of the base coat.

FIGURE 7–9. Stencil: Bricks

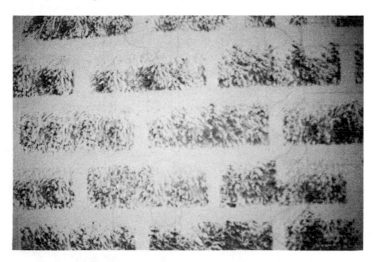

Brick stencils do not require register marks if the bricks are of a uniform size. When stencilling, the first bricks on the end of the stencil are laid over the bricks on the end of the previously stencilled area. This should line up the bricks perfectly. Charcoal guide lines should still be used to keep the rows of bricks straight.

For richer looking bricks the wall can be stencilled over in the normal way. When the stencilling is finished the dimensionality of the bricks is suggested with a series of quick brushstrokes randomly using warms or cools to break up the flat look of the wall. Next a light source is chosen. The two sides of each brick that would cast a shadow are outlined with quick, repetitive brush movements, usually with a cool glaze. The shadow below each brick is slashed with the brush in order, row by row. When all the bottoms are finished the scene painter returns to the beginning and starts again, using a vertical stroke for the side shadows. Highlights are painted in the same manner. Some bricks can be skipped at random to give the wall an uneven, textural look. The bricks can then be spattered to break them up even further. Sometimes a loose brushstroke of one or more colored glazes or of clear-flat (following the direction of the bricks) randomly applied will also increase the textural quality of the whole piece.

Variations of this brick stencilling technique can have similar applications when painting stones, tiles, and any other repeated material.

Pouncing

Another method for transferring a repeated pattern onto scenery is pouncing. Pounces are used for patterns that are not repeated frequently enough to warrant a stencil, and when reverse patterns are needed. They afford the scene painter a chance to paint quite detailed patterns, because they are actually painted with brushes once the pattern has been transferred. A pounce produces the outlines of a pattern, as opposed to the filled-in design produced by a stencil. When the pattern is transferred it acts as drawing which must then be filled in. A frieze in a Renaissance cornice is an example of a project that lends itself to pouncing.

The pattern is drawn onto Kraft paper. If the pattern is symmetrical half can be drawn on, then the paper can be folded over. It is then placed on homosote or some other soft cutting surface, and the pattern is carefully traced with a pounce wheel. This will perforate the paper, producing the pattern in a dotted line. If the paper has been folded over, the wheel will perforate both halves. In this manner, a full symmetrical pattern will be produced.

Pounce wheels come in different sizes. Smaller wheels take sharp curves more easily. Too much pressure exerted on the pounce wheel will cut a continuous line that will cut the paper apart, so care must be taken to use only enough pressure to make the spikes perforate it. After the pattern has been entirely traced the paper is turned over, and lightly sanded with medium or fine sandpaper to insure that all the holes are open.

A pounce bag is made with some porous fabric, an elastic band and some powdered charcoal. If the fabric used is very porous, as is cheese cloth, it can be folded so there are about a half-dozen layers. A pile of powdered charcoal is wrapped in the fabric, which is bunched up around it and held together with the elastic band to form a small bag. The bunched up end is used as a handle.

The pounce (paper) is carefully positioned over the scenery and repeatedly patted with the pounce bag. This releases the charcoal a little at a time onto the pounce and through the perforations. When the entire pattern has been pounced, the paper is carefully lifted off so the charcoal underneath will not smear and the excess on top of the paper will not drop onto the scenery.

After the pouncing is completed the pattern should be inked in with a waterproof marker, then thoroughly flogged to remove all the excess charcoal.

The actual painting is done with brushes. For flat-looking patterns the pounced lines can simply be cartooned over or filled in. The pattern can be painted a different color from the base coat to make it stand out a bit. For a three-dimensional look the motivating light source direction should be identified, and highlights and shadows painted in accordingly.

FIGURE 7–10. Pounce: Charcoal describes the pattern through the perforated paper.

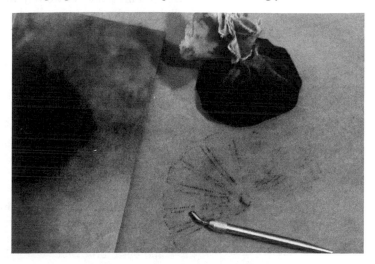

FIGURE 7–11. Pounce:
Quarters pounced onto scenery,
then painted over.

Foam Rubber Stamps

Foam rubber stamps are certainly the most enjoyable of the re-peat-pattern tools to use. Any design can be cut out of the foam rubber and almost instantly repeated hundreds of times. Patterns that must be lined up and spaced evenly are difficult to paint with stamps, but they are marvelous for freehand patterning. The main advantage to using stamps is speed of paint application. A fifty-foot foliage drop can be detail painted in an hour or less using stamps. Not only does the foam rubber have its own useful texture, but it can be nicked or cut out to form additional patterns or textures within the main silhouette. For example, veins can be cut into a leaf stamp.

To use the stamp, paint is poured onto a palette tray. The stamp is dipped into the tray so the flat bottom of the stamp is completely covered with paint. It is then stamped with a bit of pressure into a dry palette tray to remove the excess paint. This will lessen the tendency of the outline of the pattern to be sharply reproduced. It can now be applied to the scenery several times before it runs out of paint.

Stamps should be thoroughly cleaned so they can be saved after each use. If the paint dries on the stamp, that stamp becomes useless, so care should be taken to keep the stamps wet at all times until they are cleaned. With a little bit of care a good collection of stamps will accumulate after a few shows that can be used over and over again. They are a welcome addition to the paint shop, especially when a garden or forest is needed in a pinch.

Foam rubber stamps are of tremendous use for foliage painting. Painting background foliage involves entire tree shapes, where the entire forest becomes a textural pattern, and foreground foliage creates a similar texture where the leaves of each tree and bush form larger textured groupings.

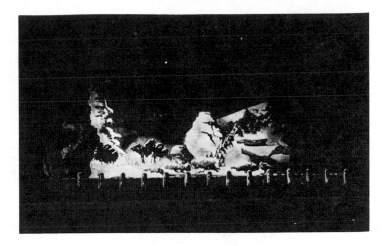

For background foliage painting the stamp should be cut to suggest the tree trunk, branches, and leafy areas. An alpine forest can be stamped from a classic Christmas tree shaped design.

The forest area should be sketched onto the scenery with light charcoal lines that delineate the boundaries, but not individual trees. The pattern can be rapidly and repeatedly stamped within that boundary. Variations can be created by only stamping the side to suggest the edge or part of a tree, the top to suggest trees in the distance or bushes, or the bottom to suggest stumps. The stamp can be dragged across the scenery to produce other textural variations.

A forest, like a tree or any other object, has its own three-dimensional shape that is defined by the way light hits it. After the basic forest has been stamped in a neutral color, it should be modeled with two or three other colors that represent light and shadow. In daylight scenes the light will be represented by a warm color. A cool color is used for moonlight. The location of the light source, be it sun, moon, streetlight, or campfire is located, and the forest is treated with light and shadow colors according to the logic of that source. This is accomplished by dipping the same stamp in the light paint, and stamping the general area "facing" the light with it. Plenty of the neutral colored trees should show through. The same is done in the dark area. An occasional dark or light tree in the main mass will suggest a tree sticking out of the forest, or a small clearing in it. By spattering and/or spraying over the forest area the illusion of distance is fostered. Such an "instant forest" can be painted in less time than it takes to build the stamp, and can make a very realistic effect on stage.

Single- or multiple-leaf stamps are used to foliate larger

FIGURE 7–13. Stamp: Greek spiral
design cut out of foam rubber.

trees in the foreground and middleground of a scene. The trunk
and branches are drawn in and painted with brushes. The leaf
stamps are used in much the same way that tree stamps are
used. Light, neutral, and shade colors will create the illusion of
three-dimensional leaf clumps. A random leaf stamped here or
there suggests randomness in nature. Using a part of the stamp
in places suggests broken or bent leaves. An uncontrolled spatter
suggests dirt, bug holes, and spots on the leaves as well as breaking up the texture to enhance the illusion of dimensionality.

Poppy fields, primrose paths, sculptured gardens, and so
on are easily created by using two or more stamps with different
colors. A flower can be created using one stamp for the flower
itself, and another for the stem and leaves. Using light and
shadow colors adds dimension to a garden, as do several differ-
ent-colored flowers.

Patterns such as Greek spirals can be applied quickly to a
set with foam rubber stamps. Charcoal guidelines are drawn or
snapped, and the stamp carefully lined up with them. A screen-
door handle screwed onto the back of the stamp affords better
control than the usual long handle. Care must be taken not to
stamp the pattern crooked, or a row will not look continuous.
The pattern should look as if it were crafted by skilled artisans,
not by inebriated slaves. Highlights and shadows applied to the
stamped pattern will make it stand out from the scenery.

The problem of spacing the stamp accurately to stamp
wallpaper patterns makes it a poor choice for that type of pattern most of the time. In some situations, however, simple patterns can be quite effective if carefully stamped at the same
angle each time, and spaced evenly along charcoal guide lines.

Bricks, stones, flagstones, and other materials can be quickly stamped onto a wall or floor. The texture the stamp affords
can go a long way toward breaking up a large expanse of floor.

FIGURE 7–14. Stamp: Ornamental spirals applied to a set.

Finally, there are also many instances when a random, unspecific pattern is wanted to simply break up an area on the floor, wings, or walls on a set. Spattering, rag rolling, feather dusting, and other texture techniques are commonly used for such a purpose. Stamps can also be used effectively. An unspecific shape is cut out of the rubber to suggest whatever textural quality is wanted. It can then be randomly stamped all over the area to be textured.

FIGURE 7–15. Stamp: Cut-foliage drop, painted in about one-half hour using foam rubber stamps.

Transfer Screen When a pattern or drawing is repeated only a few times, a transfer screen is used. The screen is laid over the drawing to be copied, and the drawing is traced onto the screen with charcoal. It is then placed back on the scenery where the repeat is to be painted, and traced with charcoal again. This time the charcoal goes through the gauze screen, leaving the drawing on the scenery, which is then inked in, flogged, and painted.

Transfer screens are also used to draw perfectly symmetrical objects. Half the object is drawn onto the scenery, then traced onto the screen. The screen is turned over, and the reverse drawing is lined up with the positive. It is traced back onto the scenery.

This method of transferring drawing works well for small numbers of repeats or reverses, but is less useful than other methods for many repeats. The charcoal tends to blur after a few uses, and the screen must be cleaned off so the scene painter can see what he is doing.

PAINTED OBJECTS Painting three-dimensional objects on two-dimensional scenery is a matter of skillfully using light and shadow colors. Five basic tones are used: shadow, shade, neutral, light, and highlight. Highlight is painted as a randomly broken line to suggest the glint of a real highlight where the light directly reflects off the object. Shadows are painted on the "plane" of the objects where no direct or reflected light hits it. Light and shade are painted on "surfaces" that are angled away from the light source or hit by indirect light. The neutral shade is the "real" color of the object.

The object should be carefully drawn in perspective. A light source direction is chosen, and all the surfaces are painted according to the logic of the source.

The neutral color (or colors) is applied first. If the object is of some material such as wood or marble, that material is worked up using the appropriate techniques. The drawing is then put on and inked over the wood, marbling, or whatever. Next shadow is put on everywhere that shadows would be. They should be distinct and unbroken. Shadow lines for straight edges must not be wavy or broken up lines. The object is worked through from shadow to highlight. The highlight should be applied last, with a light, sprightly touch. It should be a dashed line, with random length dashes that will not create an ordered pattern.

The light source that is chosen defines the logic of all the painting in a particular scene. If it is to the right of the scene, all the shadows will be cast to the left. If the source is at the center, all the shadows will be cast on the off stage sides of each painted object.

Usually a single light source is sufficient to portray depth and dimension, even though the stage lights come from many directions. A single source increases definition of the objects' dimensionality, because the shadows are distinct, and not diffused by another light source. The source should be on the same side of the stage as the key light in the stage lighting. This is the strongest light direction in a light cue. By religiously following the simple logic of where shadows would be cast if the light source and painted objects were real, the painting will make visual sense to the audience.

The same logic applies when it is necessary to use multiple light sources. One such example is a row of sconces on a wall, each surrounded by a painted moulding panel. Each sconce becomes the source for the moulding nearest it, the direction of the shadows changing at the midpoint between two sconces.

Whether a simple panel is being painted or a detailed entablature the same rules of light and shadow hold true. A plain door panel may consist of four lines. Shadow on one side and the bottom, and highlight on the other side and the top suggest a simple slanted edge panel. Reversing the shadow and highlight makes the panel appear to be recessed.

FIGURE 7–16. Painted objects: Light and shade define the molding on this flat wall panel. The same technique applies to the painted props. *The Imaginary Invalid.* Brandeis University. *Scene Painter: Robert Moody; Designer: Robert Little*

FIGURE 7–17. Light and shadow
define three-dimensionality on
flat drapery. *The Imaginary
Invalid.* Brandeis University.
*Scene Painter: Robert Moody;
Designer: Robert Little*

On detailed objects, the same principle is applied first to the object as a whole, and then to each ornamental detail on it. Some details may be completely shaded by a larger detail above them. Those that are not must be individually shaded and highlighted. Using a row of egg and darts as an example (see Figure 6-6), the shadows are put on first. The eggs cast a rounded shadow on one side, and the darts are completely shadowed on one side. They also cast a shadow onto the adjoining egg. Next, the shade color is put on the shadow side of the eggs, because the rounded objects are not completely in shadow because of their shapes and reflected light. Light is applied in much the same way on the other side of each egg, because the light is hitting it directly from that side. A neutral area is left between the shade and light colors. The same is done on the light side of the darts. Finally, highlight is put on. On the eggs it falls inside the area of light paint. On the darts it is just on the light side of the central edge. Dentals, rosettes, and other ornamental features are painted in the same way.

Sometimes there is the temptation to paint objects onto shelves of scenery when the props budget is meager. This should be avoided because it is very difficult, even for experienced scene painters. Great care must be taken if this is done, because a delicate illusion is being fostered here. Two-dimensional painted props should not be painted near places where real props will be. Attention must also be paid to the direction of the real and painted light sources. If the painted light source is imagined to be at stage right, but the real source is stage left, the highlights and shadows on the real and painted props will not match, creating visual confusion. The audience may not know what is not right, but they will sense that something is wrong. The color of the real stage light must also be considered, because it should seem to affect the colors of the two-dimensional props in the same way it really affects the three-dimensional ones.

LETTERING

Many sets include some form of lettering, and the well-equipped scene painter should be versed in stage calligraphy. Lettering appears onstage in posters (*Annie Get Your Gun*), on windows (*Bus Stop*), on signs (*Guys and Dolls*) and in many other situations. The lettering must look as if it were painted by a professional sign painter while retaining the flavor and texture of the scenery for the show.

There are several sources of lettering research that the scene painter should be familiar with. There are many good calligraphy books on the market. Inexpensive books of reprints of old posters are also available. The best sources of large numbers of alphabets and type faces are the catalogs published by the manufacturers of dry transfer lettering. Scores of alphabets are reproduced in these catalogs. They are usually distributed for free in art and architectural supply stores.

The shop should have a selection of lettering brushes in stock. Small liners are available from some of the scene-painting brush suppliers. The technique used for most lettering is less broad than that used for other scene painting. Three parallel lines are drawn in charcoal to define the top, bottom, and center of the letters. The words are sketched in, also in charcoal, paying particular attention to proportion and spacing. They are carefully checked and corrected, then inked in with a waterproof marker. After the charcoal has been flogged the letters may be painted in.

There are some stencils available for lettering on the market, but the selection of sizes and alphabets is fairly limited. Simple block alphabets are the most commonly found. When repeat lettering is required, the scene painter can create custom stencils. The lettering is carefully laid out on stencil paper, and the stencil is cut and framed. Then, the lettering is applied like any stencil with brush, sponge, and sprayer.

FIGURE 7–18. Lettering. *Can-Can.*
Boston Conservatory of Music. *Scene painter:*
Robert Moody; Designer: Harry Feiner

FIGURE 7–19. Lettering and graphics:
Magazine advertisement blown up
onto a 5-foot-by-8-foot flat. *Scene painter:*
Steven Espach. Used by permission of
James Burrough PLC and Kobrand Corporation.

156

FIGURE 7–20. Lettering and graphics:
Poster painted on a 4-foot-by-6-foot flat.
Scene painter: Lee Ann Chamberlain.
©*S.P.A.D.E.M., Paris/V.A.G.A., New York, 1983*

8

Texturing

TYPES OF TEXTURE Scenery styles demand many solutions to similar problems in different productions. Bricks, for example, may be cartooned, stencilled, stamped, appliquéd, textured out of dope, cut out of wood, carved out of foam, and so on, depending on the visual goals of a design. Some of the solutions involve painting techniques only, but many times actual textures are needed. Some of these textures, such as vacuum forming, are made in the carpentry shop. Several, however, fall within the domain of the paint shop at least some of the time.

Textured scenery is used for increased variety and visual interest. The whole look of a scene can be altered by lighting it from different angles, which is not possible with flat-painted scenery. The shadows cast by textured materials when lit from a steep angle yield a rich dimensional appearance, sometimes even making the scenery look more dimensional than it really is. Texture can be used to make scenery appear very realistic by reproducing real objects or architectural features. Realistic textured features can go a long way toward suggesting a dramatic environment in a partial setting. Texture can also be used for its own sake in an abstract fashion in nonrealistic settings to provide a gritty dramatic environment.

Textured scenery provides the most opportunities for stage lighting. Just as the texture of the weave of canvas diffuses light, materials with greater textures break light up even more. Such scenery can be lit in much the same way the actors are lit. Backlighting makes the piece stand out from the background, and sidelight and downlight make any features that stick out a lot more prominent. A lightly-textured surface lit from an extreme angle appears more deeply textured than it really is, and as such is used to create the illusion of more space.

The size of the theatre effects the way each texture reads

from the house. Burlap might produce a look in a small house similar to that of erosion cloth in a larger house. The quality of the texture must be determined for a scene, and the choice of material adjusted for the theatre size.

The main reason for choosing a texturing material is for its visual impact, but almost as important are its functional qualities. A stone wall may be made out of polystyrene foam because it is lightweight for scene shifting and easy to shape. If actors are to climb all over it, however, it might be better to construct it out of wood. A third consideration is the budget. Papier-maché and cheesecloth stones might be chosen to replace some more expensive material.

The paint shop works primarily with texturing materials that are applied to the scenery, as opposed to built-on pieces that are put on in the scene shop. These materials include textured paints and dopes that are put on in liquid or paste form, and solid materials that are put on with some type of adhesive. In addition, the scene painter is called upon to shape or texture some pliable materials and to sculpt others. A working knowledge of how each type of paint acts on each texturing substance is needed. Some paints are repelled by plastic, for example, and some paints and adhesives actually melt it. Usually these paints are not used on foam pieces unless they have been sealed with another paint first, although occasionally they are used to distress the foam on purpose.

Texture paint, scenic dope, foam, and *appliqués* are four types of texturing materials used in the paint shop. The first two are applied in liquid form, and the others are glued onto wooden or metal armatures, or onto surfaces of the scenery. Between them a range between very subtle and deeply textured scenic effects can be accomplished.

Texture Paint

Most of the time scene painters go to a lot of trouble to keep the lumps out of paint. There are times, however, when they go to some trouble to put them in. This is done when a relatively even, fine texture is to be applied to a surface.

Texture paint is exactly what the name implies: paint with some sort of texturing material mixed into it. It is fairly messy to work with. Usually it is applied with a brush, although very thick mixtures can be applied with a spatula. When it dries the bumps are very hard and distinct.

Texture paint is sold commercially for use in homes on ceilings and walls. This commercial mixture is simply sand mixed into paint. Some expense can be saved by using regular paint and putting the sand in yourself. Paint stores sell sand for this purpose, but some theatres keep sand around for sand bags, and some of this can be commandeered.

Other texturing materials are also used. One no-cost substance that creates a quite rough surface is sawdust. Many scene painters keep a few buckets filled with sawdust from the scene shop so it will be available when needed.

Heavier textural particles such as vermiculite need extra binder to be added to the paint to help hold them on. Vermiculite can be mixed up with a heavy size so it will adhere, and pigment can be added to color it.

After mixing the texturing materials into the paint, it should be tested to make sure the binder is sufficient to hold its weight. Within reason most paints will hold a good amount of texture. Some particles, such as sawdust, soak up the water in the paint, creating a lumpy paste mixture that is a little hard to work with. This can be thinned with water or some size.

Dope

While texture paint is a bumpy texturing medium, scenic dope is a smooth goo. It can be textured into, or moulded into shapes and textures, and is used for many purposes in mixtures of varying thicknesses. Scenic dope is essentially a mixture of size with a thickening agent, such as Danish whiting, in it. Pigment or paint can be mixed into it to provide color.

Thin dope may be brushed on, although care must be taken not to allow it to dry on the brush. It can be poured onto scenery and smoothed out with a foam rubber paint applicator or a squeegee. Thick dope is put on with a putty knife or spatula. As the dope begins to set up, it can be textured into with such tools as a whisk broom, wire brush, window screen, or moulded in cookie cutter-type molds. Thick scenic dope can also be applied with a cake frosting applicator, or with a plastic squeeze bottle. The frosting device can make floral designs, rosettes, and so on.

Scenic dope made of gelatin glue binder must be kept warm when it is used. The disadvantage is that as it cools it becomes gradually less pliable, and finally hard, but it has the advantage that it can be reheated to restore its pliability. Other types of dope, made from white glue or latex must be kept moist, because when they dry they set permanently. Dope mixed in the paint shop can be controlled with a little glycerine to keep it from becoming brittle. When it does it tends to crack, especially if the surface it is applied to is not rigid.

Foams

There are a wide variety of foams available for theatrical use. Most of them are commonly used for home and industrial insulation, so they are always available in one form or another at local lumber yards. Foams differ in the density and size of the particles that make them up. They come in sheets of various thicknesses, commonly one or two inches thick. These sheets are two feet wide by eight feet long. Some foams also come in blocks.

"Styrofoam" is really a brand name that refers to polystyrene foam made by the Dow company. Polystyrene foam is relatively dense and texturally consistent. Dense foams, attached to proper armatures, will support an actor's weight if necessary, although they tend to chip unless well covered with layers of some fabric like cheese cloth. A more porous foam, such as the type used to make Christmas ornament balls and cones, is easier to carve when making statuary or architectural ornamental details. Beadboard is made up of very little tiny balls of foam. It is very textural when carved, and is a very good texture when making stone walls or chimney stones.

Pouring foam is another method used to create textured or three-dimensional objects. Poured foam produces a tan-colored, relatively dense foam, smooth, but somewhat textured by the air holes produced as the foam rises. Like epoxy, it comes in two parts that rise like bread dough when they are mixed together.

Spray foam is similar to pour foam in that it comes in two separate parts. The separate canisters are hooked up to a trigger and a common nozzle. As the trigger is pulled back, equal amounts of part A and part B emerge from the nozzle, foaming up as they hit the surface of the scenery or mold. Bumpy rock surfaces can be easily created.

Appliqués

Strictly speaking anything stuck onto scenery is an appliqué. Foam shapes, wooden cut-outs, fabrics, and assorted junk all qualify. In the paint shop appliqués are usually attached with an adhesive, and are used as part of the scenery texturing process.

SOME TECHNIQUES

Each scenic design suggests applications of texturing techniques, and often creates new ones. Some of the basic textured forms are stucco or earthen walls, wood, ornamental lines such as window tracery, bricks, stones, carving and sculpture, and tiles. There are many ways to create each of these items for the stage, using several different materials. Tracery can be made with scenic dope, rope appliqué or plywood cut-outs. A gargoyle can be built up in plaster or clay, made out of papier-maché or celastic, or carved out of foam. Each technique has unique visual qualities to enhance the overall scenic style.

Texture Paint Techniques

Texture paint is the simplest texturing material to use, since it is essentially just paint. Earthen walls, or simply rough walls are

FIGURE 8–2. Carved foam and texture paint made with saw dust. *Scribes.* Set for television.

painted on evenly so the brushstroke does not break up the gritty texture of the paint. The basic wall color is used. Painting techniques such as spattering will enhance the rough look of the walls as well as adding richness to the color. Similarly, wet blends of two or three different colors of texture paint will add richness and dimension to a textured wall.

Stucco is produced by putting on the thick texture paint with circular brush strokes. This produces swirls of texture on the surface of the wall. These strokes should be randomly applied, covering the entire wall, but not creating lines of pattern on them. The technique can be varied by using different sized brushes.

Wooden cut-outs or props like pot-bellied stoves can be made to look like cast iron using black texture paint made from saw dust. This is particularly effective on fences or gates made from 1 by 1s or cut out of plywood. If gloss-latex is used, the sawdust, enveloped in its rubber paint coating, provides the requisite bumps in the iron, while the paint's shiny finish simulates fence paint.

When larger chunks of material are added to paint, they can be put on in patterns to form very rough textured objects. Vermiculite is a type of insulation material that comes in small or large chunks. The small chunks, when mixed with a strong glue size and some pigment makes a very good rough texture. A strong stencil made of upson board or masonite is cut out to represent bricks or some other pattern, and the vermiculite paint is scooped onto the stencil. The stencil is carefully lifted off the scenery so it will not disturb the wet mixture patterned on the scenery. In this way a relatively flat wall can be made to give the appearance of real bricks. Stone walls or decorative patterns are similarly formed.

FIGURE 8–3. Vermiculite applied
through a stencil makes bricks on
a hard covered flat. Foam stones
are appliquéd. *The Plow and
the Stars.* Brandeis University.
*Scene painter: Robert Moody;
Designer: Harry Feiner*

FIGURE 8–4. Finished wall
includes foams, dope textured
with a whisk broom, and appliqués.
The Plow and the Stars.
Brandeis University.
*Scene Painter: Robert Moody;
Designer: Harry Feiner*

FIGURE 8–5. Stencil cut out
of upson board, used to make a
vermiculite brick wall.

163

Scenic Dope Techniques

Scenic dope, like texture paint, provides a surface texture to scenery. This texture can be either subtle or quite broad. The subtler textures are created using light dope, or dope that is mixed thin with more water and less whiting in it. Fairly thick objects, patterns, and lines, are made using heavy dope. It is used either to make a lightweight material appear to be a different, heavier material by changing the lighter material's surface characteristics, or to simulate some object on top of the scenery.

To prevent cracking, scenic dope must be applied to a firm surface. The surface should be distressed a little so the dope will have something to hold onto when it is applied. Hard-covered flats with canvas glued onto the surface are ideal because they provide the rigidity of the plywood and the textured weave of the canvas to help the dope hold on. Dope put on soft, nonrigid surfaces will crack and chip, and possibly fall off.

Dope can be colored by adding paint or pigment when it is being mixed up. This provides a base coat which can be toned with other colors later. This is a particularly useful feature when drawing lines with scenic dope. They are so thin it would be difficult to neatly paint them after they are applied.

Stucco walls are made with dope that is put on with a putty knife. As with texture paint, the size of the putty knife, and the direction of the stroke used to apply it determines the texture or pattern of the stucco. Curved wrist movements are commonly used for this technique.

Stones, as on a wall, can be made by applying dope to areas separated by mortar lines. The mortar lines can be sketched in with a wet finger before the dope sets up. The stones can be further textured with a sponge, wire brush, or other such tool.

Three-dimensional wood grain is added to the flat scenery by brushing light dope onto the set and graining it with a whisk broom. The straw broom is dragged through the dope. Twists of the wrist produce wavy graining. A well-placed thumb makes knot holes.

Symbols, as well as texture, can be worked into scenic dope. A wall of hieroglyphics is made by writing with the eraser end of a pencil or the end of a liner handle, pushing it into the dope just before it sets up. Repeated patterns or ornamental features can be pressed into scenic dope with stamps made out of wood, foam, clay, plaster, or molded plastic. Found objects such as patterned sheet metal or molded plastic shields may be used to stamp patterns into scenic dope.

Dope can also be used for three-dimensional lining. Stained-glass-window leading or tracery is one common application. A plastic catsup squeeze bottle with a nozzle on the cap is filled with dope and squeezed out along a predrawn line. Cake frosting applicators work as well, and can produce fancier designs.

Repeat patterns in dope can be made with a stencil or a pounced pattern. Heavy dope can be heaped over a stencil. The dope must be thick enough to retain the pattern shape when the stencil is lifted off. Pounced patterns can be traced in dope from a squeeze bottle. The pounce provides the pattern guide that can quickly be traced in dope. This is a useful technique for creating fruit bowls and other ornamental designs on Renaissance entablatures and capitals.

Finally, dope can be poured into molds to produce thin ornamental features. Cookie cutters make good, inexpensive molds for this purpose. Custom molds can be sculpted out of clay. Before pouring the dope into such a mold it should be thickly greased with Vaseline. When the dope has set up, it is removed from the mold and glued into its place on the scenery.

FIGURE 8–6. Lining and cartooning in scenic dope, applied with a squeeze bottle.

FIGURE 8–7. Heavy dope applied to an ornamental railing cut-out. *Misalliance.* Brandeis University. *Scene painter: Robert Moody; Designer: Daniel Veaner*

FIGURE 8–8. Scenic dope applied
to a column with a putty
knife and textured with a
scrub brush.

Foam Techniques

Polystyrene foam is used for three-dimensional and sculpted objects. It can be carved or molded into any form, and is particularly effective when modelled with stage lighting. It is used to produce convincing three-dimensional objects, which makes it particularly appropriate in set pieces used in thrust or arena settings. Large walls, mouldings, statues, or small props may all be carved out of foam. Its advantages are that it is versatile, can be worked in several ways, and is light weight (especially important for multiscene shows). Its main disadvantage is that it chips easily, but treating it with a light coating of dope, or covering it with cheesecloth diminishes this problem.

Foam is available in lumber yards, so it is easy to find. These foams must conform to fire regulations for home building, so they may be used on stage as well. These foam sheets are reasonably priced. They can be shaped using saws, knives, hot wires, files, rasps, and sand paper.

The easiest way to shape simple foam objects is to cut the foam on a power saw. When doing this a few safety tips should be kept in mind. Safety goggles should be used because foam chips so easily, and because the gritty plastic dust from foam can scratch the scene painter's eyes. Also, the plastic foam tends to dull saw blades faster than wood does. When this happens the saw is more likely to shoot the foam back at the operator at high speed, or to bind in the blade.

Bricks may be cut out on a table saw, from sheets of one-inch-thick foam. They are then glued onto scenery in rows, leaving spaces to represent mortar lines. To provide more interest they are distressed with a wire brush, or the edges and corners are chipped and cracked.

Stones for a stone wall are similarly constructed. Layers of foam are laminated to the desired thickness with contact cement. Stone blocks are simply cut out on a table saw. The basic shape of rounded stones is cut out on a band saw. The front of the shape is then rounded off with knives and rasps.

Simple wood moulding is cut out on a table saw by adjusting the blade height for varied levels in the moulding. This limits the moulding to squared-off edges, but it is a good way to

FIGURE 8–9. Foam and vermiculite. *Artaud at Rodez.* Brandeis University. *Scene painter: Robert Moody; Designer: Michael Lincoln*

FIGURE 8–10. Light and shade paint techniques enhance the three-dimensional bricks and stones. *Artaud at Rodez.* Brandeis University. *Scene Painter: Robert Moody; Designer: Michael Lincoln*

FIGURE 8–11 (below right). Foam bricks cut on a table saw and glued onto a plywood backing.

turn out a lot of uniform moulding very quickly. Dentals may be cut out separately, then glued on at equal intervals. Pounced patterns built up in dope onto the surface of the foam add even more variety.

Curved mouldings can be cut out of foam, and layered versions such as are used in Gothic or Romanesque archways are made by cutting concentric arches out of separate sheets of foam, then laminating them.

Ethafoam rod is another type of foam that is excellent for making rounded moulding. It comes in a variety of diameters, and interesting archways, column necking, and other ornamental effects may be achieved with it by mixing different sizes together. It tends to repel scene paints so it should be covered with a sleeve of muslin or layers of cheesecloth before it is painted. For variety it can be cut in half or in quarters to produce half- or quarter-round moulding.

More sophisticated objects are made by sculpting the foam with knives or hot wires. A set of carving knives should be kept for this purpose. A large knife, a small paring knife, and a grindstone make a good starter set. The knives must be constantly sharpened because the foam dulls them very quickly. An oyster knife is also useful for gouging out chunks of foam to create a rough texture.

A hot-wire cutter can be constructed in table and hand-held models. It is basically a high resistance wire that is heated so it will melt its way through the foam. A portable version is made by taking the tip out of a soldering gun and replacing it with a loop of wire. A table model consists of a bed to hold up the foam, an arm above it to suspend the wire from, and a low voltage, high amperage transformer to heat the wire. One way to cut cornice moulding is to bend the wire to the shape of the moulding's silhouette, then push blocks of foam through it, slowly so the wire won't bend out of shape. Even with care the wire will bend and eventually break, so lots of spare wire should be kept handy. The one disadvantage to hot-wire cutting is that it produces toxic fumes. Proper ventilation is essential to its use. The scene painter should stand away from the work, and up-wind of it.

Most foam carving should be performed only after the foam has been securely fastened to its armature. The adhesive must be strong enough to withstand the pressure exerted while the carving is being done, as well as to hold the piece of foam in place.

The size of the theatre, style of the set, stage lighting and light and shade painting are all factors that determine what thickness of foam should be used for each project. Often bricks and stones will appear to be very dimensional when they are only carved out of one-inch foam. Another of the decisive factors is how much of the real object would actually stick out. Most bricks stick out from the mortar a fraction of an inch, so one-inch foam is more than sufficient for simulating bricks. Because stones are not as uniform as bricks, they protrude farther from the mortar than bricks do. Two-inch foam may be thick enough for some stone walls, but in some cases it might be necessary to laminate several layers of foam to show as much as half of the protruding stone. In any case the foam sheets should be layered before any carving begins, because the cement used to hold the layers together must have two perfectly flat surfaces in order to join them.

Thinner foam can be used when it is known that the three-dimensional quality of the carved piece will be enhanced with steep lighting angles and/or painted shadows. The steeper the angle at which the light hits the wall, the more pronounced will be the shadows it casts. Larger shadows suggest bigger objects casting them, so the illusion of thicker stones or bricks than are really present is created. When light and shadow are carefully painted on to match the angle of the real light and shadow, this illusion is enhanced even more. Of course the scene painter must be especially careful not to paint the shadow on the wrong sides of the stones.

Another consideration is that even very thin carving is three dimensional and may appear differently to members of the audience in various locations in the house. This means that in the process of carving all the views must be considered. This technique is not simply a dimensional extension of painting. When carving a stone, careful consideration must be given to the way a stone curves back into the wall. There is sometimes a tendency to try to curve the stone back, portraying part of the rear of the object, when actually the only part of the stone that would show is part of the front. At the same time enough mortar space must be left between the stones so that the stones could logically be where they are portrayed in the wall without seeming as if they must overlap each other somewhere inside the wall.

Among the many uses for foam is the simulation of cracks in walls, or deterioration of a surface edge (such as the edge of a stone fountain). When building the flats for a wall, the location of the cracks are predetermined and blocks of foam are built into these spots. The whole flat is covered with canvas, and the cracks are carved out with a knife. For making distressed edges the same sort of thing is done. A basic unit is built out of wood with foam attached to the outside edges. The whole piece is covered with canvas and carved into for a rough, crumbled-stone effect.

Stone-relief carving is another use for foam. Foam sheets are glued onto hard covered flats, and the design is drawn onto them. The simplest and crudest form of relief carving involves cutting out the spaces between the forms in the relief all the way down to the wood. This leaves squarish forms sticking out of the flat. These forms can be given a more polished look by carving into them, smoothing the edges and giving form to each object. This rough carving is a good technique to simulate cruder forms of relief. More sophisticated styles, like late Greek and Renaissance, are carved with smoother edges and more detail. Rasps and a small belt sander are useful tools for smoothly removing areas of foam.

Ornamental moulding really amounts to relief carving. The ornament is drawn onto the foam, then carved out, the negative areas removed and the positive shapes rounded off and detailed.

Another approach to relief and ornamental carving is to cut the basic shapes out on a band saw before gluing the foam onto the plywood flat or moulding. This eliminates a lot of carving, but each shape must be perfectly aligned when it is put on. The block-like shapes should be cemented onto the wood surfaces before they are carved into, so they have a firm backing and the foam will not break during carving.

The largest disadvantage to this approach is that the scenic artist is working with small details, and should keep some perspective on how they fit into the whole design. Where the audience looks is determined by the overall composition of the design, and they should not be distracted by a particularly prom-

FIGURE 8–12. Simple foam relief cut out of bead board, sealed with vinyl, and toned with spray paint.

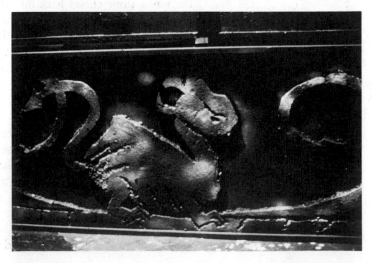

FIGURE 8–13. "Wooden ornaments" carved out of foam and covered with cheesecloth.

FIGURE 8–14. Foam ornaments fitted into an archway and painted to match wooden moldings.

inent detail. This is not to say the details should be rough or poorly crafted. They can be rough or meticulously crafted as long as they belong to a stylistic whole, and to the overall composition.

Statuary is the most detailed three-dimensional kind of foam scenery. The shape of the statue must be carefully planned beforehand so that the location of the building materials can be located where they are needed. A wooden or metal armature is built to lend strength and support, then foam is glued on where the carved parts will be. Such planning insures strength and saves materials because the foam is only put on where the carving will show. When the foam has been cemented to the armature it usually resembles a rectangular box. A front view is drawn on one surface, and a profile view is drawn to line up with the front view on one of the sides. Sometimes it is useful to draw a view also on the top. The scene painter must be able to visualize the finished object so the drawings will align properly.

Large chunks of foam are hacked off with a hand saw. This could include spaces around the head, under the arms, between the legs, and so on. The more foam that is removed in this way, the less time will be needed for the carving. The scenic artist should try to get within an inch or so of the boundary of the figure while taking care not to cut into it.

The smaller details are cut out with knives or a hand-held hot wire. When cutting out the details it is helpful to think of

FIGURE 8–15. Statue of Athena carved from foam. Sheets of foam are laminated. The form is drawn out on the foam and carved with a hand-held hot wire.

FIGURE 8–16. A wooden armature is built into the foam.

FIGURE 8–17. The finished statue is covered with a few layers of cheesecloth and sealed with latex. It is then sprayed and toned with metallic spray paints.

the original block with its front, top, and side views. As pieces are cut off these surfaces, the guide drawings should be redrawn on the foam underneath. When cutting one view, the way it fits with the others must be considered. As the foam is cut into, the figure will emerge from the combination of these views. Even so, when the scenic artist is having trouble visualizing a part of the figure it is helpful to use a human model to show how the views merge into a single form. Frequent checks should be made by stepping back to view the whole piece to make sure the form is emerging correctly and proportionally.

Column capitals, gargoyles, grotesques, and other such carved objects are made the same way. Capitals, in particular, are easy to visualize. Foam is applied to a cube-shaped armature, and the front, rear and side views are drawn onto it and carved out. Only those sides that will show should be carved. Additional ornamental moulding of wood or foam is glued on. Necking can be made by carving a ring of foam to fit around the column shaft, or by wrapping ethafoam rod around it.

Painting these objects with warm and cool colors, logically placing light and shade greatly enhances their real dimensionality. First, the appropriate basic technique for stone, marble, or metal, is painted on. The light and shade are added according to the logic of the real stage light source. After sealing the foam

172

FIGURE 8–18. The armature for this statue is built through the body into the head and arms. *The Plow and the Stars.* Brandeis University. *Scene painter: Robert Moody; Designer: Harry Feiner*

FIGURE 8–19. Two-inch foam is glued onto a wooden armature. The ornament is drawn on all four sides, then carved with kitchen knives. Wooden molding and foam necking finish the capital.

with a base coat of latex or vinyl, the foam object can be quickly shaded and highlighted with spray paints.

Foam can also be turned to produce ballisters, vases, urns, and the like. A simple method for repeating symmetrical objects in foam involves a cut-out piece of one-quarter-inch plywood and a drill press. The silhouette of half the object is drawn onto a sheet of one-quarter-inch plywood, the center line placed along an edge of the wood. This is cut out, and the sheet with

FIGURE 8–20. Coat of arms carved with knives. *The Plow and the Stars.* Brandeis University. *Scene painter: Robert Moody; Designer: Harry Feiner*

FIGURE 8-21. Foam is poured into a half-mold to make these balusters. The halves are then glued together and painted.

the negative shape is kept. The edges of the negative shape are sharpened with a file until they resemble a chisel edge.

Meanwhile, a lazy susan-type arrangement is centered on the drill press bed. The center of this must be aligned with the chuck. Nails stick up from this turntable to hold the foam. A small wooden disc with a bolt through its center (which is tightened into the chuck) has nails sticking down from it to hold the foam from the top.

A block of foam is built up or cut down to size, and inserted into the drill-press arrangement. It must be centered to the chuck, or an uneven object will result. The drill press is turned on, and the plywood cut-out is pushed onto it like a cutting blade on a lathe. (The foam turns into the blade.) A complete positive form should result.

Another form of foam to use is pour foam. It is usually poured into molds constructed in the scene shop. Large objects such as trees are poured into long molds with armatures resting inside them. Sometimes the armature is suspended in the mold with wires so it will end up in the right position inside the finished object. These molds should also be lined with waxed paper to ease the removal of the foam shape. As the foam rises it will envelop the armature. The rough trunk is then carved to make bark, knot holes, and other details.

Smaller objects can also be poured. Loaves of bread can be made by pouring foam into a greased bread pan. Cup cakes, cookies, and other delectable items, as well as ornamental architectural details can be poured in like manner. Smaller molds should be greased with Vaseline so that the forms can be easily removed without breaking pieces off in the process. The molds can be reused to produce an unlimited number of identical objects. For variety of form and texture the poured objects are carved with knives or a hot wire.

Because many foams are smooth surfaced it is often desirable to add texture on top of the foam. This is done to simulate a textured material, or simply to provide a texture to break up light as canvas does on a flat. Foam by itself must be sealed with latex or vinyl paints. This will help other paints like casein hold onto the foam, and will prevent some paints like spray paints from eating into it. A fabric applied to the foam breaks up light, and enhances its texture and the way the paint reads on it.

To prepare such a surface a few layers of cheesecloth are glued to the foam. A mixture made with equal proportions of white glue and water is used to hold it on. The cheesecloth is placed over the foam, and the size is brushed on. The fabric must be pushed down into crevices generously, because as the glue dries it shrinks the fabric, so if the fabric is not pushed down enough, it will stretch out over carved out parts, destroying their form or textural advantages. Two or three layers of cheesecloth provide a suitable surface for painting. A layer of scrim can be substituted. This is more expensive, but provides a better painting surface. Because the fabric is heavier than cheesecloth some of the finer carving might be lost. However, it will provide a more uniform texture.

Although these fabrics' textures may seem inappropriate for the materials they are portraying up close, they are not perceived as such by the audience. The texture simply serves to break up light and provide a painting surface, but it does not read as a surface texture. Wood, marble, or whatever is painted over the fabric, and they determine what the audience thinks it is seeing.

To change the surface texture as seen by the audience heavier materials are applied. Paper, muslin, or canvas maché, or heavily textured fabrics like burlap are glued on. Scenic dope can be used to augment the texture carved into the foam.

Because the foam is sensitive to some glues or paints, some interesting textures can be created by treating it before it is sealed. Spray paint and airplane glue make foam bubble and deteriorate. A rough texture can be somewhat controlled by applying a little at a time until the foam has deteriorated to the desired texture. When this texturing process is finished the piece is sealed so that no further deterioration will take place.

Appliqué Techniques

A material or materials applied to a surface is called an appliqué. This is done to produce a texture on the surface. A simple example is the canvas glued onto hard covered flats. This is put on because it provides a better textured surface for painting.

Appliqués are used to simulate very realistic objects, or can be used to create abstract surfaces and textures. Several layers of an appliqué will produce a rich, rough texture. Materials vary and, in fact, just about anything can be used: paper, fabric, wood, foam, even junk like old pipes, screen, and doorknobs. The objects in such a collage lose their individuality to become part of a richly textured surface.

Paper collage produces the flattest results. Very effective walls can be made by layering posters, newspapers, or magazine pages. Photo collages made of large blow-ups of photographs can be used to make a strong visual and thematic statement. These are applied with wheat paste to hard covered flats or other firm surfaces.

Fabric appliqués can be used to create many varied effects. A simple collage of different colored and textured fabrics will create a very rich textured surface. Different effects can be achieved by varying the color palette, and the range of texture and opacity of the fabrics. Gauzes appliquéd to a gauze drop or netting will produce varied effects when lit from different angles. Gauzes appliquéd over one another produce a watercolor-like, layered appearance.

Fabrics can easily be appliquéd to each other using a wide variety of techniques, ranging from sewing to hot-melt gluing them together. In some instances extra texture can be achieved by knotting them together.

One striking effect is achieved by applying cut-out canvas shapes, painted black, to the back of a black scrim drop. When lit from the front a black background results, but when a white drop behind the scrim is lit the cut-out pattern is silhouetted. Canvas cut-outs can also be applied on the front of fabrics or gauzes to create borders, frames, or other designs.

Another such use for fabrics is to apply strips of rags onto the scenery in the same fashion as papier-maché. The layering of these strips produces a texture of its own along with the texture of the fabric. This texture can be controlled by varying the length and width of the strips and the pattern along which they are glued down.

An inexpensive method for making a stone wall involves newspaper and cheesecloth. This works well when the materials are applied to upson-board facings that are attached to framed scenery. Newspaper "snakes" are rolled and applied to the upson board such that they describe the outlines of the stones. The newspaper is glued on with a white glue/water mixture of equal proportions. Next, pieces of newspaper are crumpled up and glued onto the insides of the stone outlines. This will add variety and depth to the stones. Finally, cheesecloth is put over the newspaper with the same size mixture. The fabric should be put on pretty loosely so it will not stretch out over the mortar lines or push down the crumpled newspaper. About three layers of cheesecloth should be put on this way. After the glue has completely dried the surface may be painted.

Sometimes foam shapes are appliquéd onto scenery. A quick and simple way to make a brick wall is to cut the bricks out on a table saw from one-inch-thick foam, and glue them onto hard covered flats. Many types of surface can be achieved in this way, including stone, pebble (foam packing "peanuts" make great pebbled texture), and ornamental designs.

Shapes cut out of wood, masonite, upson board, and many other materials can be glued onto a set. Square tiles cut out of masonite that have been individually painted might be glued onto a fireplace unit or a kitchen wall. For very realistic sets real ceramic or plastic tiles may be glued on.

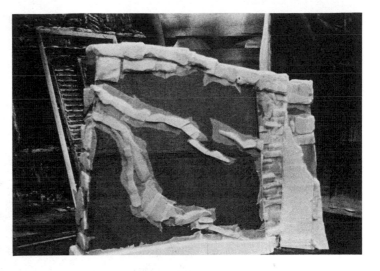

FIGURE 8–22. Foam appliqué on a
railing. *La Bohème.* University
of Missouri at Kansas City. *Designer
and Scene painter:
Harry Feiner*

FIGURE 8–23. Finished appliqué wall.
La Bohème. University of Missouri at Kansas City.
Designer and Scene painter: Harry Feiner

FIGURE 8–24. Foam appliqué, erosion cloth,
vermiculite, and dope are used in the texture
of this building. *La Bohème.* University of Missouri at
Kansas City.
Designer and Scene painter: Harry Feiner

FIGURE 8–25. Ragged erosion cloth applied over carved foam apparition heads. *Macbeth.* North Carolina Shakespeare Festival. *Designer and Scene painter: Harry Feiner*

9 Finishing the set

UNITY OF STYLE

Consistency of Style

Now that the scenery is almost finished it is time to consider again the consistency of the paint techniques employed over the whole set. The painting consists of a lot of different techniques executed by several scene painters. The charge man has overseen the individual scene painters to insure that their styles have remained consistent according to the drawings of the designer. The individual painters have been moved around to mix up individual styles, so that differences between them will mix into the general picture.

As the charge man has developed the plan of attack for the set, the color palette and techniques have been chosen to form a unified whole. Testing them on a test flat has helped to solidify the choices, so by the time the scenery has been finished everything that has been painted on it has been put on because it is part of a whole visual plan.

Style is difficult to define. It has to do with the way the designer thinks and visualizes and expresses that visualization. Articulation of the designer's vision includes the way the individual draws, chooses colors, and uses the brush. This is tempered by the designer's translation of period research, the script and the production concept for the play. All of these things, tangible and intangible, show up in the scene painting. It is up to the scene painters to make sure that these manifestations of the designer's vision come through in the painting, and that they don't get lost in a random collection of unconnected techniques and colors.

Toning

When all the techniques have been joined to produce a scenic effect they should fit together so well that they become lost in the general visual impression. No matter how skillfully this has been done the painting is still a collection of individual techniques.

179

Toning is a way to bring the techniques together into a unified visual picture. It tends to soften the brush or texture techniques in the painting, and helps create the illusion of depth in the work. Such a spray or spatter is applied lightly so that it enhances, but does not cover up, the painting underneath. Often glazes are used for toning. The toning of a set should be subtle, but the scene painter must remember that, because of the scale of the work, what is subtle to most people is invisible in scene painting. The toning must not be so subtle that it does not show.

The objectives of toning are to bring together the individual techniques already painted, to further define the composition of the picture formed by the setting, and to provide focus. Unlike many of the techniques that are painted on before, the toning covers the whole set, relating to the entire stage picture. Upper corners of the set are deemphasized so that the eye is drawn down into the set where the dramatic action is taking place. Its consistent overall application helps to relate the individual pieces of scenery to each other.

Depending on the project, a single toning spray may be sufficient to finish the scenery, or as many as four or five sprays may be needed. When applying a single spray with a pump sprayer it is advisable to apply one light spray of a color, and let it completely dry. If, when it dries, it is found to be insufficient, another light spray of the same color may be put on until that color of toning accomplishes what it is meant to do. Spraying one heavy spray all at once often results in fuzzing out the painting underneath, and in unsightly puddling and running. As this is a finishing touch, it would take a lot of work to repair such a mistake.

FIGURE 9–1. Toning with a pump sprayer defines areas of focus on scenery.

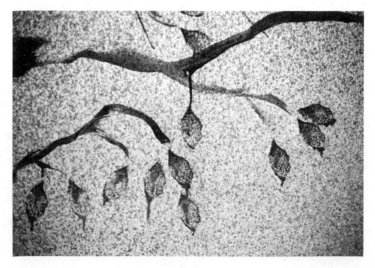

Colors used for toning fall into the categories of light, dark, warm, and cool. Light and dark colors are used to unify the color palette and techniques, and to create a sense of depth in a scene. The colors are chosen carefully, often from the existing palette. They must make sense of the blend of colors underneath, not add to the confusion. Warm and cool colors also help the illusion of dimensionality. In addition, they provide some richness of color, and something in the painting for warm and cool lighting colors to react to. This helps prevent the scenery from turning black during some light cues. Warms and cools and lights and darks are mixed as appropriate for each project. A light yellow might be used for warm toning on a set with a dark blue-green.

Of course toning will not cover up bad painting. If the base coat is too glaring, or colors in the texture techniques clash, no amount of toning will hide it. It is rather an integrated part of the scene painting process, intended to enhance the painting. The choice of colors and the consistency of the spatter or spray should be made part of the plan of action for a set, and not just tacked onto the end of the process.

In the best of all possible worlds the scene painter should be able to lay the entire set out on the shop floor in the order in which it will be assembled on stage so the whole thing can be toned at once. This would insure that all the toning is consistent throughout. In reality there is seldom enough space, so the set must be toned in sections. The scene painter should organize this so that the set may be toned in some logical order, starting with the units from one side of the set, and moving across to the other side. If several sprays are used they should be put on in the same order on each set piece, to insure that each part of the scenery will be consistent with the other parts. The last section that was sprayed should be kept in view as a model for the next section.

Toning can also be used to help provide focus to the acting areas and other important areas. Heavier, darker toning in the upper side corners of the set will draw the eye down to where the actors are on the floor. Such toning should not cover up the painting in these less visually important areas, but should provide a gentle suggestion that brings the eye down to lighter areas below. The lighter areas are chosen for their dramatic importance, as well as visual logic, and they should gradually fade into the areas of darker toning.

This approach to defining large areas of light and shade using toning can be used in a general sense, or very specifically to enhance the portrayal of motivated light sources such as windows (sun or moonlight), chandeliers, and lamps. The technique becomes especially important in theatres with limited lighting equipment. Toning on the set can suggest lighting effects such as sunlight from a window hitting a wall, or the spread of light from a lamp, thus freeing the real lighting instruments for use in the more important acting areas.

Painting the Floor

The floor can be either an extremely important or insignificant element of a set. Its importance is determined by how many people in the audience can see it, and how much of it is seen by them. Often the architecture of the theatre is the deciding factor, where the variables are the rake of the auditorium, the size of the balcony, sight lines, and so on. A raked stage automatically increases the importance of the floor. When much of the floor is seen by many people it becomes an important scenic element, and must be painted with as much care as any other part of the set.

The floor has two characteristics that are different from those of the other parts of the set. First, people walk on it. This obvious fact has important implications when choosing colors and the type of paint to use. The second is that virtually all the stage light hits the floor. If, for example, a show is hung with one hundred instruments, each lamped at five hundred watts, and even if the average intensity of the dimmers is one-half there are still twenty-five thousand watts of light, most of it hitting the floor.

Actually, people do more than walk on stage floors. They run, scuff, drag themselves and other objects across them, and (worse!) tap dance on them. Because of the excessive wear a floor must endure, paint with a strong binder should be chosen to cover it. Latex and vinyl paints are commonly used, as opposed to caseins, which are better used on walls and drops.

The value of the floor colors is affected by both wear and stage lighting. Scuffing and dirt will change the apparent value of the color, while the stage lighting will seem to lighten it considerably. In general, it is wise to darken the value of the floor color by a few shades so it will appear consistent with the colors on the rest of the set, and so it will be less reflective of the light, and therefore not a distraction. With experience it becomes possible to gauge how much darker the floor must be to compensate for lighting, and how much brighter to compensate for wear. Generally, the effect of lighting is greater than that of wear. Thus, floor colors should always be at least a shade or two darker.

The lighting designer prefers the darkest possible floor color to absorb as much light as it can. Light bounces off lighter-colored floors, spoiling tightly controlled lighting effects. Thus, a darker color choice not only improves the look of the floor, but is a technical necessity for the lighting.

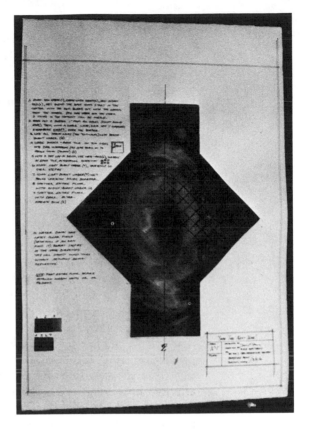

FIGURE 9–2. Painter's elevation for a floor. A blend is indicated underneath, with details painted over.

Finally, the type of painting technique to be used must be considered. Generally, a broader technique can be used on the floor. Most of the audience sees the floor at an angle, which somewhat distorts what they are seeing. Again, the idea is the audience may be given the impression that they are seeing a particular type of floor, which may or may not be what they are actually seeing. Very precise details may not show up, or even may form an unwanted pattern. A much broader technique should be used in larger theatres and, in general, the floor technique may be broader than that used on the walls of a set.

Real Painted Objects

Along with flats, drops, and other large set pieces, the scenic artist is called upon to paint smaller objects such as furniture and props. Most of the same techniques as are applied to large scenery are used on these smaller pieces, but on a smaller scale. The scale of the technique that is used should be scaled to the size of the object being painted, but in such a way that it remains integrated with the rest of the painting on the set.

When choosing the techniques with which to paint furniture, the following goals should be considered:

1. Simulating a specific material.
2. Enhancement of three-dimensional aspects of the piece.
3. Believability of the piece within the context of the whole scene (style of painting).

One should never just "paint a chair." The chair is supposed to be made out of something specific, and it has to have an identity in the context of the rest of the scene. It is made of a certain type of wood that is finished in a particular way. Even passing attention to such details will enhance the credibility of the entire dramatic environment.

Almost nothing on stage should be painted simply in one flat color. Even a richly carved chair can be enhanced by toning of some kind. This might be in the form of a spray, spatter, or some other style, such as mottled brushstrokes of warms and cools in a dry blend following a grain.

The style of painting of the furniture must not only be believable for the individual piece, but must also fit in with the painting style used in the whole scene. This is not to say that the furniture should fade into the background. It must seem as if it belongs in the scene. Furniture and props are as much a part of scenery as flats and drops, and as such must be integrated. No matter how beautifully a chair is painted, it will be less effective in a scene, if not glaringly distracting, if it has not been considered as an integral part of the scene. For clues about color and style, the scene painter should look at an actual piece of furniture made in the desired wood. Some of the veneer companies provide samples of prestained woods, as do many furniture manufacturers.

Very convincing "stained" wood furniture can be created using the same techniques as on door mouldings, but with some minor modification. Everything is scaled down. The areas of color in the wet blend are smaller. They are still randomly placed, but painted on more neatly. The graining is also more precise, and special care must be taken to avoid blobs of paint at the beginning and end of each brush stroke. After all the painting is done, including spattering and toning, the entire piece is painted with clear latex or vinyl. This brings the colors back out so they read as if they were still wet (a couple of shades darker, and brighter). It provides a shiny, varnished look. Also it seals the piece so water and other liquids can be sponged off without harming the paint job. While clear-flat is used on scenery, furniture should have something of a shine to it. Clear semi-gloss provides enough shine, without causing a distracting glare.

Some furniture is simply spray painted. Some examples are ice cream parlour chairs and lawn furniture. More visual interest

FIGURE 9–3 (above). Simple cartooning
on a stylized chair

FIGURE 9–4 (top right). Table painted
with casein paint and finished with
polyurethane to simulate stained wood

FIGURE 9–5. A mock-up of a baby grand piano
painted with wood techniques

is afforded such furniture if it is toned after it is covered with the basic color. Light spraying of a warm color from one side and a cool color from the other will increase the audience's perception of its depth. On heavily-sculpted chair backs, the toning colors should be held close to the furniture surface, and sprayed across it so the paint catches under the ridges in the carving, thus reinforcing the relief. A lot of furniture has very interesting relief carved into it that will not read unless it is reinforced in this manner. This is simply a matter of letting the three-dimensional carving do the work for you. A quick spray brings out a design that may otherwise have taken hours to complete.

Individual styles suggest the appropriate techniques. The light-colored Renaissance-style furniture might be base coated in a cream color, then toned with warm and cool pastels with the brushstrokes following the direction of the grain. Gilt parts are put on using bronzing powder, and a spatter of metallic paint can add a rich quality. When this is done, a coat of clear semigloss finishes the job.

FIGURE 9–6. Chair with real carved relief.

FIGURE 9–7. The relief is toned with spray paint to emphasize the real carved design.

FIGURE 9–8. Painted plastic leaves appear
to be real. *Scene painter: Robert Moody*

Because furniture for scenery comes from so many different sources—stock, rented, borrowed—it is sometimes necessary to match several different pieces to a piece or set of
furniture already finished in a particular way. This is difficult,
unless the scene painter is somewhat skilled. It is easier to paint
all the furniture, determining the style and avoiding having to
match colors and texture techniques.

Prop foliage is another item that should be dealt with by
the scene painter. A dry blend of paint not only provides a
depth and richness of color, but also eliminates the fake-looking
shine that most plastic foliage has. Again, even very good foliage
may look out of place onstage unless it is integrated with the
rest of the set. The color palette and style should be consistent
with that of the other scenery. Spattering goes a long way toward making three-dimensional foliage look real. It provides the
inconsistencies that occur in nature that are not included on
mass-produced plastic leaves.

Paper foliage may be dipped in a bucket of base-colored
paint. A production line of leaf dippers can produce a virtual
forest in very little time. All the leaves are laid out on the floor
and, after they have dried, are broadly spattered.

Other props must also be dealt with in terms of the overall painting plan. Everything on the stage should present a single unified picture, and exceptions will distract from the main
action in the drama.

Once the set has been moved into the theatre, a new set of problems arise. While the paint shop is arranged for the convenience and ease of scene painting, the stage is often the opposite. Once the set has been assembled, parts of it become inaccessible, and it is difficult to maintain a consistent style over large areas. Thus, it is best to have as much of the set as possible, if not the whole thing, painted before the put-in.

Even under the best of circumstances the painting is not perfectly finished before the set leaves the shop. In the course of moving it, pieces get nicked and scratched, and wear caused by actors during rehearsals and performances will necessitate maintenance of the paint job. There are also some items that cannot be painted until the show moves into the theatre. For example, if the set does not include a deck, the stage floor must be painted or treated in some way.

Touch-ups maintain the freshness of the painting and the frequency of touch-ups depends on the use of the set. Most short-run shows only need one touch-up before opening. A dance musical might need weekly touch-ups. By opening night it is pretty obvious what will be needed in the way of touch-ups. At this point a decision can be made as to which paint, if any, needs to be saved for subsequent touch-ups.

The safest way to match colors in a touch-up session is to save the colors originally mixed for the set. This can be successfully accomplished over short periods of time (two or three weeks). The best container for saving small amounts of paint is a plastic freezer container with an air-tight lid. This retards evaporation of the paint medium by keeping it out of the air. Larger amounts, kept in buckets, should be checked on every day or two. About one-quarter-inch of water should be added to the top of each bucketful of paint, but not stirred in. Covering the bucket with a plank also helps to retard evaporation, and prevents dust, dirt, and kamikaze flies from contaminating the paint. If the paint is saved for several days, each bucket should be stirred once a day, and a new layer of water added on top.

All the main colors used in the set should be saved. If an area of the set is touched up, the original techniques have to be matched so the retouched area will not stand out. This may mean that everything from the base coat up has to be done exactly as it originally was. The base colors should be saved in the greatest quantity. Smaller amounts of each of the other colors are usually adequate for the requirements of a minor touch-up.

One task that can be counted on is the touching up of heads of nails used to assemble the set. These must each be dabbed with paint so they will not reflect light. The best way to find all the nails is to turn on all the stage lights, and view the set from all over the house. The nails will show up quite clearly. A small liner and some base or blend color will make the nails disappear. At the same time, chips taken out of the set by missed hammer strokes can also be taken care of.

The main difficulty in a touch-up is maintaining the consistency of the techniques used in the original painting in the shop. Spattering and spraying, so easy in the shop, can cause more harm than good to the assembled set unless the parts that should not be sprayed are masked off. The auditorium and the stage floor also must be kept clean. Still, it is important that these steps not be skipped or the touch-up will not match. This may mean spending more time masking off an area than it takes to paint it, but this must be done. Using a less messy technique instead of the right one (like sponging instead of spattering), just covers one bad patch with another one.

When painting the set pieces in the shop it is a good idea to be aware of which joints will show on the assembled set. Edges of flats that will show should be based and all the other techniques used on the walls in the shop as the pieces of scenery are being painted. This will be greatly appreciated during the touch-up because it saves a lot of ladder work. It is also difficult to blend a complicated series of techniques over a three-quarter-inch-wide vertical strip of wood with those painted on the front of the flats. Tasks that are very simple in the shop, such as matching a wallpaper pattern along edges of flats, can be very painful experiences on stage.

Another odd item that must be touched up is bracing. Presumably the facings will be perfectly fitted. When they are not it is helpful if the light-colored wood that braces them does not glare through the cracks. Such bracing should be painted the set's base color, or black to make them disappear from view.

Areas of the stage floor that are not covered by the

FIGURE 9-9. A scene painter blacks out platform bracing.

ground cloth or a deck, or that are not masked by the set or curtains also need to be painted. The usual scenic convention is that if something is black, it is not there. Thus, the stage floor should be painted a flat black. The black, contrasted with the ground cloth, will help define the acting area and the composition of the set design, plus it will absorb spill light. Flat black latex is usually used because it is inexpensive and durable. Some theatres use vinyl or black surface stain. When a set has no scenic floor treatment, the entire floor is painted black. Sometimes a designer will choose brown instead of black to soften the contrast between the set and the floor. To control light reflection a dark color should always be used.

CLEANING UP

Cleaning up is the final step in painting a show. A lot of the clean-up chores are performed from day to day, and if this routine is kept up the final clean-up does not take very long.

What to Save

Since it is unlikely that the scene painter will be able to guess to the ounce exactly how much paint to mix for a set, the probability is that there will be left-over paint. Once paint has been opened, it does not last very long, but there are some things the scene painter can do to extend its life. A judgment has to be made considering the possible future use of each color. Is there enough left over to be used on another project? Is the color likely to be used again soon in its current form, or for mixing other colors? If the answer is no, then the color should simply be tossed out.

Some shops that are constantly painting shows maintain slush buckets. All the left-over blues are poured into one bucket, all the browns in another, and so on. The resulting colors are used for mixing, back painting or (in educational theatre) low-budget laboratory shows.

Organic paints go bad fairly quickly and, although they may still be alright for painting, they exude a pungent effluvia. This can be retarded, although not totally avoided, by storing the paint in air-tight cans, and also by adding a little bit of household disinfectant to the paint. Aside from the olfactory benefits this affords, the shelf life of the paint is increased.

As paint cans are emptied during the mixing process, some of them, with their lids, should be cleaned and put aside for future storage of leftover paint. A helpful trick is to puncture the rim of the can a few times with an awl so the paint will not collect in the rim, but will drip through it back into the can. This saves paint, and makes it easier to get an air-tight seal when the lid is put on.

Used paint should be stored on the thin side because its

exposure to the air makes it more likely to dry up. Some water should be stirred in thoroughly so the paint will not settle into a hardened cake.

Special tools such as stencils and stamps should be cleaned and saved. Stamps are invaluable for many uses and should be kept in good shape. If a stencil has made it through a show in more or less one piece it could be used on a hall backing flat in a future set some time.

Very specialized pounces or foam molds should be tossed out unless there is some definite prospect for their reuse. Cheap brushes used for glue and cement can be discarded too if the glue has hardened on them.

Cleaning Equipment

A lot of shop heads and scene painters who own their own painting equipment are fanatical about keeping their brushes and other tools clean. Proper cleaning takes only a few minutes, but often brushes, sponges, and stamps are left sitting while paint dries hard on them. Once the paint has hardened in such a tool, it is ruined. The bristles in a brush cannot be restored, and the pores in a sponge are filled forever. Tools that have almost dry paint stuck in them are salvageable, but only after much work, and they may never regain their full capabilities.

Today scene-painting brushes cost between three dollars and one hundred dollars a piece. Natural sponges are expensive, and foam rubber stamps take some time to build. The few minutes it takes to care for a brush are more than worth it when measured against the brush's replacement cost.

During the paint call, used brushes and other painting tools should be submerged in a bucket of clean water. The water should be changed several times during the day. When the scene painter cannot tell whether the contents of the bucket is water or paint, it is time to change the water.

Brushes should be cleaned and put away at the end of each paint call. They should be thoroughly cleaned in cold or luke-warm water. Hot water melts the glue in the ferrule, causing part or all of the bristle bundle to fall out. Sometimes the cleaning is speeded up by using bar soap in the bristles, but this is not necessary. The brush should be filled with water, then flicked hard as it is when spattering. This forces the paint toward the end of the bristles by centrifugal force, and speeds up the cleaning. When a brush looks clean it should be tested to make sure. It is filled with water. The water is allowed to run out into the scene painter's clean hand. If only water comes out, the brush is clean. If there is any paint mixed in the water, more cleaning is needed.

White-bristled brushes retain some paint color in the bristles (black bristles do too, but you can't see it). This does not necessarily mean the brush is not clean. Some paint colors have dye color in them that stains the bristles. The brush is definitely clean if, when filled with water, no paint runs out.

Bristles may be trained to retain their original shape. The best way to dry a brush to facilitate such training is to hang it from its handle, bristles down. If the bristles have bent out of shape, or if some separate from the main bunch, the brush should be wet and the bristles smoothed into shape. They should then be carefully wrapped in a wet paper towel and hung up to dry. When the towel is removed after the brush has dried, the bristles should maintain their proper shape. Brushes that have been left to dry in a bucket with their bristles down will be trained to curve, due to the weight of the brush above the bristles. They can be retrained using the paper-towel technique. If a brush cannot be hung up to dry, it should be placed in a can with its handle down to protect the bristles from bending. A little hand lotion massaged into the bristles will also help to train the brush.

Foam rubber stamps and sponges are cleaned similarly. They are repeatedly filled with water and wrung out, until nothing but clear water comes out. This is particularly important, because if paint is left in these tools it will harden, rendering the tools useless.

Feather dusters are cleaned like brushes, taking care not to squeeze the feathers too hard so they do not break. Yardsticks and straightedges should be wiped off with a wet towel.

Pump sprayer tanks should be rinsed out with warm water two or three times. Then they should be filled with water and pumped up. The trigger should be locked on so the tank will spray continuously until clean water emerges from the hose. The pressure is let out, and the tank is rinsed once or twice more. Pump sprayers should not be stored with the pumps locked in them. When the seal dries the pump could stick to the tank. Pumps should be stored separately, or loosely placed in the tank.

Finally, the counter tops and other surfaces should be wiped off. Counter tops can be recovered with Kraft paper so they will have a new surface when the next show is begun. Paint should be securely stored, and buckets containing mixed colors should be relabeled.

Glossary

ANILINE DYES. Brilliant, transparent colored dyes. Used instead of paint for translucencies and brilliant scenery.

BACKDROP. (See Drop.)

BACK PAINTING. Usually black or gray latex or rubber paint used to black out or opaque scenery.

BASE COAT. The first coat of paint (after the painting surface has been prepared) in scene painting. Usually of the color dominant in a piece of scenery.

BINDER. Glue or other substance which adheres pigment to the surface being painted.

BLENDING. Painting areas of color that do not mix to form a new color, but fade into each other at their boundaries (wet), or meet at their boundaries (dry).

BRONZING POWDER. Metallic pigment in powder form.

BRUSH. A tool used to apply paint to a surface. The bristles are held onto the handle by a metal ferrule. The bristles distribute the paint consistently as the paint runs along them to their ends.

CARPENTER (GROUND) GLUE. A strong, inexpensive glue that comes in powder form. It must be mixed with water over heat.

CARTOONING. Drawing outlines of shapes on scenery, similar to the drawing used in comic strips.

CASEIN. A protein that is one of the chief ingredients of milk. It is used as a binder in paint. Nowadays a soy substitute is used in many brands.

CHARGE MAN. The head of the paint shop.

193

COLOR. The property of light reflecting specific wavelengths from the visible spectrum. Colors are divided into earth colors and dye colors. Some standard earth colors: yellow ochre, red ochre, raw sienna, burnt sienna, raw umber, burnt umber, black. Dye colors: lemon yellow, golden yellow, orange, red, magenta, purple, cerulean blue, turquoise, ultramarine blue, navy blue, emerald green, chrome oxide green.

COMPLEMENTARY COLORS. Colors directly opposite each other on the color wheel.

CUT DROP. (See Drop.)

CUT LINES. Painted lines separating painted objects such as tiles or planks.

DECORATING BRUSH. (See Fitch Brush.)

DEXTRINE. A binder that comes in powdered form. Used for bronzing powders and prevents analine dyes from running.

DISTRESSING. Beating up a piece of scenery (or a prop) to make it look old and used. Also, painting a texture onto flat scenery to make the painted object seem battered or weather beaten.

DRAWING STICK. A bamboo stick flayed at the end to permit the insertion of a charcoal stick. When the end is wrapped with an elastic band it prevents the charcoal from falling out. Used for drawing on scenery laid out on the floor so the scene painter does not have to stoop to draw.

DROP. An expansive piece of fabric scenery suspended from above. A backdrop is the rear-most drop in a scene. Other kinds of drops are cut drops (with areas cut out, and netting applied to support cut-out areas), sky drops (usually white or blue to represent an undefined area of sky), and translucent drops (painted on both sides). (See also Translucent Drop.)

DRY BRUSHING. Dragging a brush lightly over scenery so that the individual bristles leave paint marks instead of a solid brush stroke.

DYE COLORS. Colors produced synthetically, or with mineral pigment. Greens, blues, violets, oranges, some yellows, and reds. (See Color.)

EARTH COLORS. Colors made from natural pigments; ochres, siennas, umbers, some reds, some blacks. (See Color.)

FEATHER DUSTING. Stippling scenery with a feather duster.

FEATHERING. Lightly stroking an area of wet paint outward with a brush to produce a soft, feather-like edge.

FERRULE. A band of metal that contains the bristles (and the glue that holds them together) on a brush, and connects them to the handle.

FITCH BRUSH. Large liner. Brushes with natural bristles that taper out from a flat, trapezoidal ferrule. Comes in sizes from one inch to three inches. Also called Foliage Brush or Decorating Brush.

FLAG. The split ends at the end of each bristle on a paint brush. The flag helps to distribute paint evenly onto a surface.

FLOG, FLOGGER. A device consisting of several strips of canvas or muslin attached to a handle. Used to erase charcoal from scenery.

FOLIAGE BRUSH. (See Fitch Brush.)

GELATINE GLUE. Glue in powdered or crystal form made from animal hooves. It must be broken down with water over heat.

GLAZE. Paint mixed very thin so that colors and drawing underneath show through.

GLUE POT. A double boiler on a stove for melting down powdered or crystal glues.

GRAIN. The natural disposition of a material such as wood, marble, or stone. Also, a texture in wood. "Painting with the grain" of an object means that the brush strokes go in the direction of the implied grain of the painted object, usually along its length.

HOLIDAY. A spot accidentally missed when applying a coat of paint.

HUE. The distinctive characteristic of a color.

INKING. Drawing in a design in ink. Usually done with a dark-colored waterproof marker so the design will show through layers of paint as a guide to the scene painter.

LAYING-IN. Painting a base coat or other large area of color.

LAYING OUT. Drawing the design on scenery.

LINER. A small brush with a long handle, used with a straight-edge for painting lines. Comes in several sizes from one-quarter-inch to three inches. Some liners have flat ferrules, and some have round ones for lettering. (See also Fitch Brush.)

MEDIUM. A liquid that permits the pigment and binder to spread easily onto a surface. When paint "dries," the medium evaporates, leaving the pigment and binder on the scenery.

MOTIVATED LIGHT SOURCE. An imaginary light source (such as the sun or a street lamp) that dictates the placement of light and shadow on two-dimensional painted scenery.

OPPOSITE COLOR. (See Complementary Color.)

PAINT. A mixture of pigment with a binder and a medium.

PAINT FRAME. A large, motorized wooden frame that rises and descends through a slot in the floor, against a wall in the paint shop. Tall scenery is fastened to it so the painter does not have to climb ladders or scaffolding to reach it.

PAINTER'S ELEVATION. Frontal view of scenery painted as it would be seen under work light. Usually painted on illustration board in one-half-inch or one-inch scale.

PIGMENT. Coloring matter in powdered form.

POUNCE BAG. A porous fabric bag filled with powdered charcoal. Cheesecloth or lightweight muslin is commonly used. (See Pouncing.)

POUNCE WHEEL. A small, spiked wheel attached to a handle on an axle that is used to perforate craft paper for pouncing. (See Pouncing.)

POUNCING. Transferring a pattern onto scenery through paper that has been perforated with a design, by patting the paper with a pounce bag. This causes powdered charcoal to go through the perforations, leaving the pattern on the surface underneath.

PRIMARY COLOR. A color that cannot be made by mixing other colors together. In pigment: red, blue, and yellow.

PRIMING. The coat of size, sometimes mixed with whiting and/or pigment, which stretches and seals scenery fabric.

PRIMING BRUSH. A large brush, seven to twelve inches wide, used for priming and base coating.

PUMP SPRAYER. A device for spraying a mist of paint. A hand pump is used to build up air pressure in the tank, which pushes the paint through an adjustable nozzle. These sprayers are manufactured for the purpose of spraying chemicals on foliage to exterminate pests.

PURITY. The measure of saturation of a color.

PUT-IN. Assembling a set on the stage.

RAG ROLLING. A texturing technique involving the rolling of a twisted rag that has been dipped in paint over scenery.

READ, READING. The way scenery is perceived from the house (auditorium). Example: a pattern of light dots reads as fog or mist. A technique that creates a desired effect reads well.

SCUMBLING. Painting with random brush movements in different directions.

SECONDARY COLOR. A color made by mixing two primary colors in equal proportions. In pigment: green, orange, violet.

SIZE. A mixture of medium and binder.

SIZE BARREL. A barrel kept in the paint shop that holds several gallons of working size.

SIZING. Applying an even coat of size to a drop or flat to stretch and seal it. (See Priming.)

SKY DROP. (See Drop.)

SNAP LINE. A length of twine that is coated with charcoal or chalk so that it can be stretched and snapped to produce a straight line on scenery.

SPATTERING. Creating a "texture" of dots on scenery by flicking paint off a brush. Best accomplished with a priming or lay-in brush.

STARCH. A food substance found in corn, potatoes, and the like that stiffens fabric. Corn starch and laundry starch are used for sizing scenery.

STENCIL. A design cut out of heavy paper, framed for use in scene painting, when a pattern is to be repeated.

STENCIL BRUSH. Short, stubby, round-ferruled brush, used to stipple through stencils.

STIPPLING. Patting scenery with the ends of the bristles of a brush, or with a sponge or other scene painting tool.

TEXTURING TECHNIQUE. A scene painting technique that produces what appears to be a texture on flat scenery. Texture techniques are two-dimensional, not actual textures.

TRANSFER SCREEN. A large (at least 2-by-2 foot) framed piece of scrim for exactly copying a drawing or pattern from one part of a set to another.

TRANSLUCENT DROP, TRANSLUCENCY. A drop thinly painted on both sides. When lit from the front the scene painted on it shows. When light from behind is added the colors and shapes painted on the rear show through. This technique is often used for sunset effects.

VALUE. The black to white relationship of a hue.

VINYL. A compound derived from ethylene that is used as a binder in paint.

WHITE GLUE. A white, premixed glue made from dairy products. Can be diluted with water.

WHITING. A thickening agent that comes in powdered form.

WORKING SIZE. Size that has been mixed in the correct proportions to make paint.

Index